WEST TO EDEN

Texans in Hollywood

DONALD CLARKE

EAKIN PRESS ★ Austin, Texas

Published in the United States of America
By Eakin Press, P.O. Box 23069, Austin, Texas 78735

ISBN 0-89015-617-4

Library of Congress Cataloging-in-Publication Data

Clarke, Donald.
    West to Eden.

    Bibliography: p.
    Includes index.
    1. Moving-pictures — California — Los Angeles — History.   2. Hollywood (Los Angeles, Calif.) — Biography.   3. Texas — Biography.   I. Title.
PN1993.U65C56   1987   791.43′092′2   [B]   87-13675
ISBN 0-89015-617-4

For Tara, Troy, and Amanda,
the brightest stars in my constellation.

Contents

Preface

"The fascination with Texas lies in freedom. . . .
I was taught since birth, that if you were from Texas, you could do anything you wanted to do. . . .
The more places you go and have to compare to Texas, you realize those things aren't bragging statements. They're true."
— Willie Nelson

A contemporary of Willie Nelson, I grew up hearing the same things he did, and feeling much the same way. As a result, while camped on the salty Brazos River during my fifteenth summer, when the light from our campfire had died down some, I confided to a boyhood friend that I intended to become an actor in Hollywood. It wasn't dark enough to tell him that my desire stemmed from having fallen in love with a young actress who appeared in her first film that summer, and the only way I could see to get her was by becoming an actor. Her parents were screenwriters in Hollywood, and she had been named for her godmother, Texan Joan Crawford.

Instead of hooting and howling at my outrageous ambition, he said quietly, "I believe you can do whatever you want to."

A few years later I was at home in Hollywood with a beautiful actress wife, a hard-working agent, and television and film roles to my credit. I had married into a Hollywood family with strong film connections, and the talk when we were together usually centered on movies and the people who made them. Some of the stories in the following pages I heard for the first time at those family gatherings. Running through the tales was a cable of respect — awe, almost — for Texans. That didn't seem unusual to me at first, having grown up hearing how male Texans were a foot taller and ten times stronger than mere mortals, and the women were always more beautiful and talented than those born elsewhere. I know now that that reputation is exaggerated. Slightly.

But the aura is derived from accomplishments, not talk. A roll call of the biggest stars, directors, and writers in Hollywood's history includes an astonishingly large number of Texans. During the centennial celebration of Hollywood's founding, it seems an appropriate time to look at some of the Texan contributors to the history of one of the few places in the world that compares with Texas in terms of legend and mystique.

There is a dark side to great accomplishment, and Texans, unfortunately, are not immune to it. Their stories cover ten fabulous decades of the Four Horsemen of Hollywood: ruthless ambition, scandal, heartbreak, and the crowning glory of triumph. In the long run, it is triumph that dominates.

Recalling Texan Don Meredith's words, used in another context but applicable here: "If you do what you say you'll do, it ain't braggin'."

Acknowledgments

I owe a debt of gratitude to Sherrye Ann Lewis, who listened to these stories many times on our walks through the countryside, then read them with a fresh perspective nothing short of amazing.

I'm also grateful to the Academy of Motion Picture Arts and Sciences for their cooperation, to Larry Edmonds Bookshop, Hollywood, for photographs, and to Michael Price for help in updating the list of Texas artists.

A Star in the West
Beckons Texans

One might legitimately wonder why so many Texans achieved prominence in Hollywood. After all, in the early days of motion pictures, Texas was largely a rural state. Artistic accomplishment usually is associated with the city. Where did these marvelous stars and directors and writers get their inspiration and training? What special attributes allowed them to triumph? And what lay on the far side of paradise for them?

It all began with the dreams that men and women have always had of achieving success through magical means. For centuries they have embodied those dreams in myths, adventure stories, and fairy tales. Nothing epitomizes the modern fairy tale so well as Hollywood.

After the turn of the century, movie stars represented a new kind of hero in America. They did not reach astronomical heights because they possessed Horatio Alger characteristics of diligence, honesty, and purity of heart. Rather, they were known to be spendthrifts and given to profligate behavior. Yet they were among the most highly rewarded individuals in the world in terms of material success and fame — ironically, in a society whose ethos rested upon hard work and virtuous deportment.

The public got to see these individuals at work, earning all that fame and fortune. The waitress compared herself with the heroine on the screen; the shoe clerk matched himself against the hero. Soon the dreamer would say: "I could do that . . . I'm no different from them . . . it could happen to me."

No other industry in this country besides rock music advances such uncomplicated and easily accepted invitation to the ego. And even though they may not currently look like movie stars, viewers know that actors have *their* blemishes corrected by makeup, lighting, orthodontia, or surgery. So could they.

How many stories have been read of discovery against almost incalculable odds? A movie magnate has a flat tire — the would-be star happens along the deserted road in time to fix it and is discovered. Or she wins a watermelon-thumping contest, bringing her to the attention of important people. These things do happen. Even more bizarre but genuine stories of discovery are recounted by potential stars to fortify their courage. Fame and fortune do come overnight when the right person is in the right place. All it takes is luck. Not talent. Not preparation. Not training or connections. Just luck. A very appealing philosophy to the young.

Movies are one of the few enterprises left in the world in which high rewards are promised to youth; in which youth is an advantage rather than a burden. Inexperience is of little account. The aspirant needs no investment capital, no skill, no background in the field. An attractive face or scintillating personality may be enough to put one's name above the title of the film.

In truth, breaking into Hollywood is usually no more difficult than running a sub-four-minute mile. In hobnail boots. On an August day in Texas. And the odds against success are about as long as late afternoon shadows in the California sun.

But it has happened to several who had their beginnings in a rural state called Texas.

During the first two decades of this century, Texas was a state consisting largely of small communities, villages, and hamlets. That meant limited entertainment sources. All it took to show a film was a dark place, chairs or benches, a sheet, and electricity. People were used to gathering for camp meetings and church services, so when a motion picture came to town, they knew how to get there. Many movies were shown at night in tents or in the open air, using a portable generator to run the projector.

Dispelling the loneliness of isolated frontier living, the flickering images were a godsend to rural dwellers, and admission was cheap. It is not surprising, then, that motion pictures gained almost instant acceptance in the wide open spaces of Texas. Filmmakers could scarcely have conjured a more receptive audience. And it was through these makeshift theaters that the early Texas artists gained inspiration to try out Hollywood.

As with so many other things in modern life, Thomas Edison made Hollywood possible. Early in 1893, he exhibited publicly for the first time a coin-operated peephole machine called the Kinetoscope. Only one viewer at a time could see the world's first moving picture, but the novelty proved successful enough to lead Edison to manufacture a total of 700 Kinetoscope machines. They were sold to penny arcade managers across the United States and in Europe. The machines showed films of only fifty feet or so, lasting less than a minute, but a demand was generated for new film production.

To satisfy that demand, Edison created a "motion picture" department of his company and erected a building in West Orange, New Jersey, to make motion pictures. The "studio" was called Black Maria, in reference to the tarpaper covering the building. The subjects of films made at Black Maria were vaudeville performers from New York City, performing bears, dog acts, and artists such as Sandow the Strong Man, Carmencita the Spanish Dancer, and Annie Oakley, Little Miss Sure Shot.

By 1894 Edison had perfected a projector that threw photographic images onto a screen. The basic invention had been patented by Thomas Armat, but Edison persuaded Armat to join his company. He correctly believed that the name of Edison would sell more machines than the name of Armat. Together they marketed the improved projector as the Edison Vitascope.

Vitascope projectors were available for commercial use early in 1896, and eighty sold very quickly. Purchasers became exhibitors, and they spread across the country to show the wonders of film and to make some money. Richard Paine and Robert Balsy ended their Vitascope tour of the West in Los Angeles, undoubtedly bringing the first motion pictures seen on a screen to that city.

A man named William N. Selig operated a traveling minstrel show in the Southwest. He ended his 1894 tour in Dallas, where he saw the Kinetoscope in operation at a penny arcade. When he returned to Chicago that winter, he immediately began building a camera and projector. Selig became one of the first, if not the first, producer of a film shot in Los Angeles a few years later.

Of more immediate moment, a man named Thomas Lincoln Tally from Waco also saw the Kinetoscope in Dallas and right away perceived the far-reaching commercial potential of the machine. Son of a rancher, Tally had been a cowboy, typesetter, and hardware salesman before he obtained rights for the sale of Edison's phonographs in Texas. He bought six Kinetoscopes and had them delivered to Los Angeles. In August 1896 he opened the "Phonograph and Kinetoscope Parlor" at 311 South Spring Street. The peep machines were lined up in a row, and a viewer could go from one to the next for a different one-minute film.

Not long after he opened, Tally bought one of the Vitascope projectors from Balsy and Paine, and he promptly renamed his business the "Phonograph, Kinetoscope, and Vitascope Parlor." A picture of Tally's place shows the Kinetoscopes and phonographs in the foreground, and in back, a cloth partition used to darken the area where the projected movies were shown. The cloth contained peepholes for patrons who were afraid to sit in the dark during daytime. The regular admission fee for viewing a Vitascope film was ten cents; some say peepers got a free look, others that Tally charged them fifteen cents for the privilege. The latter seems more likely in view of Tally's slick business practices, seen later when the stakes were much higher.

In April 1902 Tally moved his company, now called Electric Theatre, over a couple of blocks to 262 South Main Street. In a front-page advertisement in the *Los Angeles Times* dated April 16, 1902, the "new place of amusement" offered "UP-TO-DATE, High Class moving picture entertainment. Especially for Ladies and Children." (Tally is credited with coining the term "moving pictures.") For ten cents, patrons could see the capture of the Biddle Brothers, New York in a blizzard, and "many other interesting and exciting scenes" lasting an hour altogether. The Electric was a real theater, seating 200 viewers.

The next year, when he got a copy of Edwin Porter's *The Great Train Robbery,* Tally's theater was full every day. Guessing that a film like that would not come along every month, Tally closed the Electric Theatre and took the twelve-minute Porter film on tour throughout the West before returning to Los Angeles to reestablish a permanent theater.

The Wacoan was, to say the least, an enterprising entrepreneur, and he played a most significant role in the structure of the movie business after World War I. He sold his empire in 1928 and took up cowboying again on his ranch near San Bernardino. But this time he was a rich cowboy. And he kept his wealth, unlike some of his motion picture friends who were wiped out by the crash of 1929.

From 1896, when Tally arrived in Los Angeles, until 1906, moving pictures turned into moving stories — physical action stories rather than stories of deep emotion, but narratives, nevertheless. The next ten years produced lasting motion picture elements, most of which still exist today. The decade produced the feature film, the film star, the premier distinguished director, the first picture palaces, and the wonderland known as Hollywood.

William Selig, after working up his own camera and projector and becoming a film producer, sent a production unit to California from Chicago to shoot exterior scenes for his film *Monte Cristo,* in late 1907. Other producers followed, responding to the enticement of West Coast weather. They could shoot outdoors all summer and, except for a few days, all winter. Interior scenes could be filmed outdoors as well by using muslin overhead to diminish or eliminate sharp shadows.

In addition to the accommodating climate, California and adjacent states offered limitless variations of seacoast, islands, mountains, valleys, countryside, desert, and plains, for the setting of any story. Westerns, that early staple of Hollywood fare, could be shot without leaving Los Angeles County. Also tempting producers westward were lower labor costs — anywhere from twenty-five to fifty percent lower than in New York. And perhaps more important than all the other attractions put together, the independent producers had some distance between them and the Motion Picture Patent Company, which sought to restrict severely the use of patented equipment made by Edison and others.

Selig's representative had rented the back part of Sing Loo's Chinese Laundry, on Olive Street between 7th and 8th streets in downtown Los Angeles, for his studio. But to the north and west, land was advertised for sale in Hollywood: "Choice building lots in The Holly Tract at $150 to $400 per lot on easy terms." This advertisement by the R. W. Poindexter Company, from about 1905, shows that land was extremely cheap not far from Hollywood and Vine. The land, covered with orange and lemon groves, was a parcel carved from extensive ranch holdings of Mrs. Deida Wilcox, the wife of a Kansas City real estate man who had bought the large ranch in 1886. Soon the land was divided into smaller units. In 1903 the community was incorporated as a village, keeping the original name of the ranch — Hollywood. The village continued to grow, and in 1910 it was annexed by Los Angeles so that the smaller community could hook up to the city's water supply and sewage system.

This general area became attractive to the film producers who had followed Selig because it was inexpensive, had plenty of room to expand, and allowed the moviemakers to cling together as a "colony" in a somewhat hostile social environment. The locals didn't like them and didn't want them in their community, at least initially. Posted above many vacancy signs was the strict condition: "No Jews, actors, or dogs allowed." As one legitimate-theater man, Oliver Morosco, noted at the time: "Those locusts are swarming into Los Angeles, building ramshackle studios from the beach to the mountains. Literally thousands are trekking west and this is resented by large groups of people, mostly churchgoers, who are forming committees to keep these ragtags and bobtails off the streets and out of our parks. These damn flicker outfits have even built more nickelodeons! Which are filled to the rafters."

The last two sentences are the key to Morosco's outrage. After the colonists had been established for a while, however, Morosco, seeing the enormous sums of money that could be made, became part of the movie industry himself. His son Walter also became a producer and intimate friend of Texan silent superstar Corinne Griffith.

A few weeks after Morosco made his observation, a committee calling itself the Conscientious Citizens had obtained more than 10,000 signatures on a petition to drive the invading army of film people from their midst. Fortunately for Hollywoodites, nothing ever came of the drive, and the natives soon discovered that even movie people needed to buy homes, clothes, food, and services.

When profit entered the relationship, film folk received an enthusiastic welcome.

Early producers were quick to take advantage of the beautiful and varied scenery provided by the West Coast environment, and as these scenes flashed on screens in cities and hamlets across the land, individuals responded to the magic. Alone, sitting in a darkened theater with the drab reality of their lives shut out, many young people were transformed into the stars they saw before them, and there could be no keeping them on the farm or ranch after they had seen California. They packed their bags and headed west.

Most of the popular screen heroines were still in their teens, and the girls watching them could readily see themselves taking their places. If they didn't, frequently their mothers did and bundled them up along with the family belongings for the journey to the promised land. Others had their travel and rent paid by parents who were sure their progeny were prettier than current stars like Mary Pickford, Dorothy and Lillian Gish, and Marguerite Clark. Many of the girls came alone, willing to pay the price to get into the studios. Few were talented, and the frustrations they experienced trying to break into film faded their youthful prettiness rather quickly. They were turned away each day unless a mob scene was being shot. Hunger took its toll; despair made them vulnerable to unscrupulous men who advanced them enough to live on. When older, more experienced actresses advised these unfortunate young women to return home, they were rebuffed with taunts that indicated the older women, who were in their twenties, were merely jealous of the newcomers' youth.

The young men who traveled west seeking fame on the screen took defeat more philosophically. If they could not get on as actors, they became studio crew members or looked for jobs in restaurants or business offices. None wanted to leave the glamorous setting of Hollywood.

But in spite of the influx of jobseekers, *talented* actors and actresses *were* wanted and needed. Some of these clever young men who possessed fine skills in discovering cinematic potential created a demand for their services by becoming "scouts" for the studios. They were paid for locating and bringing in gifted actors and actresses. They called themselves "agents," and by the 1960s they controlled the motion picture industry.

One impressionable viewer of early films was a teenager who lived in Galveston. Son of well-to-do parents, he was eager to earn his own way, and at an early age he landed a job taking tickets at a Galveston moviehouse called the Globe Theater. The hours were long, from 10:30 A.M. until 10:30 P.M., and the ticket taker also relieved the projectionist for lunch and dinner breaks. During the twelve hours of theater operation, he saw the same film twenty-four times. Since the program did not change for several days, the youngster became intimately familiar with every frame of every film, and he made a conscious effort to learn how different effects were achieved. He became critical of the story line, the camera work, the acting, and the directing, and he decided to become a director himself. The youngster, King Vidor, achieved his goal by becoming one of the top Hollywood directors before he reached thirty.

Vidor attended Peacock Military Academy in San Antonio after high school, which he "detested," and he made several film shorts and documentaries in and around Galveston. One day, as he and a friend from the academy were walking along Main Street in Houston, the friend pointed to an exceedingly attractive young woman riding in an open touring car and wanted to know who she was. Vidor was not acquainted with her, but he soon learned her identity. She was Florence Arto, soon to become Florence Vidor. Fortunately, she yearned to be a film actress as much as he wanted to direct, and they planned to storm Hollywood soon after their marriage.

The young filmmaker made several documentaries of news and commercial appeal, including one for a Houston sugar company. After all the bills were paid, he and Florence had enough left over for the down payment on a Model T Ford that carried them to California in 1915. Vidor was then nineteen years old, Florence seventeen.

Several summers before he left for California, Vidor met a hauntingly beautiful young girl named Corinne Griffith while visiting a famous health resort in West Texas called Mineral Wells. Vidor spent time with Miss Griffith, a Texarkana native, and found that she too had been bitten by the movie bug. At the Airdome Theater, Vidor and Griffith nudged each other as they noted particular exciting effects on the screen. They had reached a "professional" understanding.

Six months later she wrote to Vidor in Galveston, asking for a letter of introduction to anyone he knew in Hollywood who might be able to help her get a start. Vidor remembered a distant cousin who was married to a stage comedian then living in Santa Monica. He wrote the letter, and the comedian introduced Miss Griffith to the head of Vitagraph Studios. Impressed with her exceptional beauty (she was to the silents what Hedy Lamarr was to the talkies), the director-general guaranteed her two days a week at $5 per day, and for each day beyond the two, should she be needed.

When King and Florence Vidor arrived in California, they immediately made their way to the door of Corinne Griffith's Santa Monica apartment. Corinne later introduced Florence to the head of Vitagraph, then operating out of Pacific Electric's freight station near Santa Monica Canyon. The head man moved Corinne to a three-day-week slot and put Florence in Corinne's old two-day slot. With $10 a week coming in, the young couple could scrape by.

King Vidor began writing scripts, which he attempted to sell to Vitagraph or Inceville studios, also located in Santa Monica. In addition, he did newsreel and travelogue photography and any other studio work he could get. He wrote fifty-two motion-picture scenarios before Vitagraph finally bought one.

During a long rainy spell, all shooting had practically shut down and the studio needed to utilize expensive actors and directors on the payroll. Vidor's story could be shot entirely in the rain: it was called, appropriately enough, *When It Rains, It Pours*. He received $30 for it, and he never told whether he wrote the script before or after the rain started.

Vitagraph quickly outgrew its cramped facilities in Santa Monica, and when the studio moved to Hollywood, the Vidors moved too. Corinne was promoted to stardom and Florence to the vacated three-day-week position.

The Vidors' first Hollywood home was in a boardinghouse a short distance from the D. W. Griffith lot at 4500 Sunset Boulevard. Griffith was shooting *Intolerance,* his great follow-up epic to *The Birth of a Nation.* Griffith had spent $100,000 to build just one set for *Intolerance,* more than he laid out altogether to produce *Birth of a Nation.* The set was so huge it had to be built outside the studio proper, across the street in an open field. Walls of canvas were erected to keep out onlookers, but Vidor managed to get inside.

And on Sundays when Griffith wasn't shooting, the young Vidor inspected the set thoroughly, studying, learning.

A player in the film being shot was another Texas-born beauty, Juanita Horton. Born in 1898 in Midland to a cowboy father and schoolteacher mother, she got her start in the movies in 1915 while still a student at Los Angeles High School.

Having missed an appointment to see Tom Mix at his studio about working in one of his Western movies, Juanita was advised by Mix's studio to see D. W. Griffith "if you want to go into pictures." She took a streetcar to the studio on Sunset Boulevard and asked to see Griffith. Frank Woods, head of the scenario department and longtime associate of Griffith, interviewed the young woman. The famous director happened to pass by, and with his ever-alert eye for nubile beauty, saw her and questioned her motives. She was innocent and honest: her family had little money, were in fact, she said, living in poverty, and she needed a summer job. "Mama said I wasn't trained to do anything, so there was nothing left for me but acting."

Griffith held his laughter in check and told her to report after lunch for a test. He led her through an improvisatory scene in front of seasoned veterans on the set and she passed the test, winning the featured part of the Bride of Cana in the Judean episode of *Intolerance*. But before she appeared in that film, Griffith saw to it that she got leading parts in other Triangle productions, of which he was a third part. She appeared in several films starring William S. Hart and Douglas Fairbanks before Griffith shot her scenes for *Intolerance*. For the early work she was put on a contract at $10 per week, but by the time of *Intolerance*, she earned more than double that amount.

Before Juanita Horton finished her first movie, the studio changed her name to Bessie, because even a child could pronounce it, and Love, because the studio wanted everyone to love her. Other actresses of the day were called Ailene Pretty, Blanche Sweet, Louise Lovely, and Alice Gentle, so one sees the reasoning.

Shortly after her appearance in *Intolerance*, a critic described Bessie Love as "the sweetest, demurest, tenderest, most plaintive little thing on the screen." No one could argue that she *wasn't* little: five feet tall, 100 pounds. But after her tenure as a sweet and demure heroine for Griffith, she moved on to a career as a fine dramatic actress in the twenties.

Meanwhile, King Vidor learned from Griffith, and he made the rounds of all the studios seeking work as an actor, assistant director, propman, cameraman, or assistant cameraman. At last, Universal hired him as company clerk for $12 a week; his duties were to keep accounting records of the unit to which he was assigned. There he saw inept directors whose talents were so mediocre they gave rise to the criticism, "The picture is so bad that they have to make retakes in order to keep it on the shelf." He was more certain than ever that he had the talent to be a good director, but he had to wait awhile and busied himself in the interim by writing scenarios, some of which sold. Florence Vidor was, at the same time, well on her way to becoming one of the most popular stars of the day.

At about this same time, a convent-educated young woman arrived in Hollywood who would ostensibly cause the Vidor marriage to lose its sap. Colleen Moore was the niece of Walter Howey, editor of the *Chicago Examiner*. D. W. Griffith owed Howey a favor for helping *Birth of a Nation* and *Intolerance* clear the censors, so Griffith repaid the debt by giving Colleen a chance in films.

King Vidor eventually wrote a full-length script that interested a group of doctors, surprising because of the obvious Christian Scientist bias of the story. *The Turn of the Road* contained a lot of antimedical material, but the doctors set aside any prejudices they may have had and put up $9,000 for Vidor to make a movie from the script. For his original story and scenario, Vidor would be paid $200 after the $9,000 had been repaid to the doctors, and he would be paid $100 a week to direct the film, payable in $60 cash and $40 deferred until later. Vidor would have done the film gratis; he needed a feature film to his credit.

The young director finished the film a few dollars under budget, and it opened at Quinn's Rialto, a bankrupt theater in downtown Los Angeles. After almost three months, the line of people waiting to see the movie still extended half a block into a side street. There was only one copy of the film, and the doctors wanted to take it to New York for national distribution. With Quinn's theater in the black for the first time, it took a deputy sheriff to pry the film loose from him. The distribution company gave Vidor and Brentwood Film Corporation, the doctors' organization, a $10,000 cash advance. The $9,000 movie eventually grossed over $365,000.

A return of $40 for every $1 invested starts your telephone ringing. All at once stars such as Dustin Farnum, Clara Kimball Young, and Mary Pickford wanted him to direct them. Suddenly King Vidor was a feature director, but he felt a debt of loyalty to the nine doctors and he resolved to stay with Brentwood for a year, even though no contract with them existed. The corporation expected him to write all the original stories and scripts, as there was no money in the budget for the purchase of story material. The Texan wrote and directed three more films for Brentwood in 1919: *Better Times,* starring a new discovery of his, Zasu Pitts; *The Other Half,* starring his wife Florence; and *Poor Relations,* also starring Florence Vidor.

His moral obligation discharged, Vidor established his own studio, Vidor Village. He began to produce his own films for release through First National, a producing-distributing organization that was the brainchild of fellow Texan Thomas Tally, who by then was a major exhibitor headquartered in Los Angeles.

Vidor's legendary love affair with actress Colleen Moore in the early 1920s eventually caused his divorce from Florence. He was divorced twice more, but found himself reunited with Moore after his retirement in 1959. They remained close friends until his death in 1983, at the age of eighty-eight.

The most popular silent star, after Gloria Swanson and Pola Negri, was born in Dallas on January 14, 1901. Bebe (Phyllis) Daniels was the daughter of a Scottish-born father and Spanish-born mother. Her father managed a touring theatrical company starring her mother, and by the time she was four, Bebe regularly appeared in their plays. She made her film debut at age nine in a Selig company two-reeler called *The Common Enemy* and played many child roles in other short films, mostly adventure stories and Westerns. By the time she was fourteen, Bebe began playing adult roles in two-reel Hal Roach comedies that usually starred Harold Lloyd and sometimes Australian comedian Snub Pollard.

Hal Roach had opened a studio in 1914 in the old mansion owned by Lewis Bradbury, located on Court Street above the Hill

Street tunnel in downtown Los Angeles. Roach built a stage in the back yard and used the horse stables to store props. This was a typical beginning for many studios — taking an old home built by an early settler and converting it into a "studio." The larger rooms became offices, while living quarters became dressing and makeup rooms. Roach's studio was known as the Rolin Film Company, and Daniels co-starred in some 200 short comedy features there from 1915 to 1918, including most of the "Lonesome Luke" *(Stop! Luke! Listen!)* and "Winckle" series with Lloyd.

Perhaps the most popular Hal Roach production was "Our Gang," which featured a little Texan. George Emmett McFarland, a pudgy toddler born in Dallas in 1918, became a model for a Dallas Bakery at age two. A year later he replaced Joe Cobb as the fat boy in the "Our Gang" series. In all, he appeared in eighty-nine of the two-reel episodes, but Roach claimed he was too valuable to use often. Roach made more money loaning the youngster out to other studios for feature films than he did from using the boy called "Spanky." McFarland was easily the best known of all the players in the series that is probably more easily recognized by TV audiences under the reissue title of "The Little Rascals."

While Bebe Daniels was playing in Harold Lloyd comedies, she and Lloyd frequently could be seen dancing after work at the Sunset Club, the Alexandria Hotel, the Ship Cafe in Venice, Nat Gooden's, or the Pier in Santa Monica. Very special occasions were celebrated at the Vernon Country Club. Dance contests were popular events at all these places, and Bebe and Lloyd usually walked away with the trophy.

One night they were spotted in a Hollywood restaurant by Cecil B. De Mille, who recalls in his autobiography, "that's how Bebe started making feature-length films." She played a spicy favorite of the Babylonian king in the flashback sequence of Jeannie Macpherson's adaptation of *The Admirable Critchton.* She was eighteen, and her career as a major star began. Paramount quickly rushed her into a second picture, *Everywoman,* a film version of a modern morality play. Bebe symbolized Vice. "There has never been a Vice," according to *Photoplay*'s film critic, "on stage or screen, so gorgeous or glittering as Bebe Daniels."

At about this time, Lloyd asked Bebe to marry him, but she refused. She wanted a marriage to last, and Lloyd had a wandering eye. He reportedly sired more illegitimate children than any other star in the history of Hollywood. Besides, she enjoyed going out with heavyweight champion Jack Dempsey and other eligible young men. According to Adela Rogers St. Johns, who lived, loved, and worked in Hollywood several decades, "I'd have to say that Bebe Daniels was the best-loved and most all-around popular girl who has ever been in Hollywood at any time. . . . she came to represent to us all that is finest in an American girl — and woman — though early on she got herself into more trouble than most! And that for a number of reasons. Among them the fact that so many men fell in love with her."

Once while on a personal appearance tour in the Midwest, Bebe's jewelry was stolen from her hotel suite. The next day it was returned on the personal orders of Al Capone, her secret fan. Such was the appeal of this Texan.

Mary Pickford's brother Jack fell madly in love with Bebe, and perhaps she with him. Mary summoned her image from the past: "I can remember her better than anybody. No matter how . . . casually or for how short a time . . . anyone who even so much as met Bebe Daniels, remembered her always afterwards with . . . vividness. Some people, maybe most people, you have to stop and bring them back so you can see them and sometimes you never quite do. But Bebe is always there just as she was. She and Jack were . . . so wonderful, so happy together."

Fortunately, no matter how "happy" she may have been, Bebe had good sense. She turned Jack down, and he married Olive Thomas, a well-known actress of the day. They hit it off well; both enjoyed drugs immensely, as well as alcohol. Olive died of a dose of poison in Paris at the height of her fame in 1920, disappointed when she failed to score a big stash of heroin she had planned to have on hand for Jack's arrival the next day. Pickford himself eventually died at thirty-six, the result of dissipation.

In 1919, then, Bebe Daniels had signed what turned out to be a long-term contract (ten years) with Paramount Studios after she got her start in the De Mille features. She typically played impish, warm, often comic, light leads. Less frequently she played hardened, experienced playgirls. The five-foot-three actress had black hair, brown eyes, and 112 pounds nicely distributed, which enabled her to play successfully a variety of roles. Among her leading men were Wallace Reid and Rudolph Valentino.

But Bebe was different in one major respect from her twenties' peers. Her publicist, Wilson Heller, recalled, "Among my women clients — and I mostly handled women — it was well-known around the business that only a few of them never laid a guy to get where they were: among them Bebe Daniels, Lois Wilson, and Patsy Ruth Miller. They would go to parties now and then, but they wouldn't screw. They weren't on the make. Most of the others got their jobs by laying somebody. Among the early stars, I think every damn one of them laid some guy to get ahead, or further ahead after they got started." If Heller is correct, it's a wonder De Mille signed her.

In 1923 Governor Pat Neff asked Bebe to come to Texas to promote cotton products. The cotton industry was in a severe slump that year, and Daniels gave her hearty support by touring throughout the state.

She became experienced in all aspects of filmmaking. At age twenty-four she had complete supervision of her film unit: stories, casts, and budgets. Of the twenty-five pictures she wrote or co-wrote, Paramount had to turn down only one story. She was the only woman among a group of twenty top directors and writers on Paramount's inner cabinet. But when sound came to films, Paramount refused to give her a voice test. Perhaps they were simply tired of her; it happened to actors all the time. At any rate, they offered her the opportunity to work out the last six months of her contract as a writer. Confident of her abilities, she refused and bought up her contract.

She went over to RKO and talked William LeBaron, head of studio production, into giving her a voice test. He recalled seeing her and Bessie Love sing and play the ukelele at parties, so he decided to go ahead with the tryout. Her cousin, Dr. Lee DeForest, supervised the sound test. He was the inventor of much of the technology used in putting sound on film. Bebe succeeded admirably and was given the starring role opposite Texan John Boles in *Rio Rita*. Daniels proved she could not only talk but could sing as well. The film was a popular and critical success and was one of the first sound musicals. (Bebe's friend, Bessie Love, starred in the first, MGM's *Broadway Melody*.)

Daniels finally found the right man when she was thirty. He was Ben Lyon, one of the stars of Howard Hughes's *Hell's Angels*. The marriage would last forty-one years, until death did them part. The Lyons went on tour to England in 1935 and finally took up residence there. When World War II broke out, they sent their children to America and stayed in England to fight the war. Ben was an air force pilot who returned to active duty. They both served the interests of the U.S. by entertaining American soldiers during the war, and Bebe was the first civilian woman to enter France after the invasion. The United States government later awarded her the Medal of Freedom for "her unselfish services and willing sacrifice under the most dangerous conditions."

Not many actors who were already stars on Broadway could be tempted to try films. The new medium was an upstart, audiences could not hear the dialogue, and the product was aimed at illiterates, as compared with highly literate New York theater audiences. But as films gained stature and salaries became astronomical, actors began to have second thoughts.

Cecil B. De Mille and his brother William had Broadway backgrounds and had earned respect for their theatrical skills. It was somewhat easier for them to recruit stars from the stage than for directors and producers whose total experience consisted of films. One Texan who succumbed to their blandishments was Elliott Dexter.

Dexter, handsome leading man of the silents, was born in Galveston in 1870. He spent many years in vaudeville and on the stage before going to Hollywood to star in numerous screen productions for Cecil B. De Mille and other directors. He became known as the quintessential De Mille star, playing more leads (eleven) for De Mille than any other masculine star. Listed among his leading ladies were such luminaries as Gloria Swanson and Mary Pickford. He and Swanson became especially close, and she looked to the older actor for advice and mature friendship.

"Elliott Dexter must have sensed that I was out of my depth when I first arrived at Paramount," remembered Swanson. "I was clearly not used to making pictures with real jewels and real roses any more than I was used to being treated like a duchess by a director who behaved and spoke like a sultan. Elliott, on the other hand, had been a star for years and moved with perfect ease in that land of dreams, and he obligingly made a point of going ahead and clearing a path for me each time a new type of scene came up."

Dexter was happily married to his frequent co-star in De Mille films, Marie Doro. The stunning beauty was an "English" actress who had been born in Pennsylvania. On one early occasion, when the couple took Miss Swanson out on the town to a club called the Ship Cafe, "within an hour, half of the people there had stopped by our table to say hello to the Dexters."

De Mille asked his favorite scenarist and lover, Jeannie Macpherson, to write a scenario called *Something to Think About* (1920) especially for Dexter. The movie was a piece of markedly religious sentiment about "a lone man's frustrated and embittered but finally victorious search for love," a different kind of film for De Mille. Perhaps it was a personal expression; he usually sought stories that exploited sexual themes. Elliott Dexter clearly was a De Mille spokesman on screen in many of their films together.

Dexter made twenty-one films from 1915 to 1919 and another twenty from 1920 until he retired from films in 1925. He was known as a dependable actor who could be counted on for a solid performance in whatever role he was cast, and was one of a very few movie actors who retired of his own volition.

The Sedgwick family from Galveston had made their way to Hollywood by 1917 and began appearing in films made there. Edward, the oldest (born 1892), and his twin sisters, Eileen and Josie (born 1895), started their show business careers as children in circus and vaudeville acts with their parents (The Five Sedgwicks). Edward and King Vidor had collaborated on two one-reelers in 1914 back in Houston that came to nothing, but Edward Sedgwick was determined to become a director, a goal he achieved in the twenties. He appeared as an actor in several movies before he got his chance at the helm of a film production for Universal.

Josie, Eileen, and Edward got their start in films with Sigmund ("Pop") Lubin, the German-born pioneer film executive. The Sedgwicks had worked for Lubin briefly before the company's bankruptcy in 1917 sent them to California in search of further film work. Eileen gained popularity as the heroine of numerous Universal serials and played leading-lady roles in many shorts before turning to Westerns in the twenties. Josie also played in serials before the twenties, when she became leading lady to silent cowboy stars Art Accord, Hoot Gibson, and Buck Jones.

Another Lubin alumnus was Edwin Carewe, born in Gainesville in 1883. Carewe (real name, Jay Fox) became a stage actor while still in his teens. Deciding on a career in films, Carewe spent a few months bumming around the country as a hobo before joining Lubin as an actor in 1910. Typical of the period 1914–1916, when there was a surge in the recruitment of directors, actors frequently stepped behind the camera and took over direction of a film. This was the case with Carewe, as with the overwhelming majority of directors who made their first films before 1918. Carewe wrote the last film he acted in for Lubin, *Across the Pacific* (1914), then moved to Metro, where over the next five years he directed numerous films. He also began making pictures for Pathé in 1919 before joining Associated First National in 1921 as a director-producer.

There was still another Texan who performed brilliantly in films and began his film career with Lubin. Tom Forman was born on a ranch in West Texas in 1894 and attended The University of Texas. He acted, directed, and wrote scenarios for Lubin and then Universal Studios. The blond, handsome young man served as a lieutenant in the army during World War I before returning to an active film career. He directed many films for Famous Players-Lasky (Paramount) before turning freelance, and he earned a well-deserved reputation for turning out top commercial films. His last film, *Devil's Dice,* was released October 31, 1926. He suffered a nervous breakdown, and while recuperating at his parents' home in Santa Monica he put a gun to his head. He died November 26, 1926.

Edwin Carewe's cousin, Wallace Fox, was born across the border in Purcell, Oklahoma, but his roots were in Texas. He attended the Military Academy in San Antonio at the same time as King Vidor. After leaving school, Fox started his career as a black-face entertainer in Isley's "Lone Star Minstrels."

After a short stint in vaudeville, Fox broke into films as a propman in 1919. Later, in honorable Hollywood fashion, he worked for cousin Carewe as an assistant director. In 1927 he got his own opportunity to direct, mostly low-budget Westerns and action pictures at Monogram. He also directed a few films at RKO and Universal. In the forties he directed many East Side Kids (Bowery Boys) comedies, and in the fifties, he moved over to the small screen.

Carewe's brother, Finis Fox, collaborated with the director in writing some of Carewe's best films, including *Ramona* and *Resurrection*. However, the coming of sound put an end to Carewe's career, despite his success with silents. Not much was heard from Finis Fox after that.

One of the better writer-directors to come from Texas was Rian James from Eagle Pass. Born in 1899, he had acquired only a grammar school education before he became columnist for Walt Whitman's old newspaper, *The Brooklyn Eagle.* After seven years at that post, he became a foreign correspondent for the International News Service. When he returned to the United States, he was a newspaper reporter, parachute jumper, and stunt man. He also became a lieutenant in the First Division Air Corps, then an air mail pilot and vaudeville actor.

James authored fourteen books of fiction and three nonfiction books. In addition, he served as official historian of three British East Africa archaeological expeditions. Among his numerous screenplays was the ground-breaking *42nd Street,* starring Bebe Daniels, Ruby Keeler, Ginger Rogers, and Dick Powell. Daryl Zanuck hired him specifically for the task. At the time, audiences were tired of musicals, but James did such a masterful job on the script that interest was revived in the genre.

One Texan who was not a writer, director, or star nevertheless achieved great Hollywood fame. He was A. A. "Buddy" Gillespie, from El Paso. Gillespie, born just before the turn of the century, attended Columbia University and the Art Students League. He became involved in films in 1922 and served as art director for MGM from 1924 until 1935, when he took over as head of the company's special effects department. Altogether, he had hundreds of films to his credit, and he won four Academy Awards for his efforts. Gillespie provided special effects for *San Francisco, The Good Earth,* and *The Wizard of Oz,* among other films. Developing the cyclone sequence in *Oz* proved one of his greatest challenges, Gillespie admitted at the conclusion of his long and illustrious career.

Another Texan contemporary with Gillespie was Travis Banton from Waco. Banton also attended Columbia and the Art Students League, but his interests lay in clothing design. While still a student (1917), Banton met Norma Talmadge, who was making a movie in New York. She commissioned him to design one of her costumes for the film, but aside from one other brief assignment,

Banton did not work for the movies until 1924, seven years after Talmadge gave him his first chance.

Paramount Pictures called him to California, and his Hollywood career began with a picture called *The Dressmaker From Paris,* starring Leatrice Joy. It was a perfect start for a designer; the star needed dozens of fashionable outfits for a fashion show, and naturally, the fan magazines played up the beautiful dresses and gowns. Typically, Paramount's publicity department claimed Banton was from Paris, France, not Waco, Texas. They could have saved their ink, for within a few years, Travis Banton's designs had a much larger audience than that of any French dress designer. In the twenties he created lavish wardrobes for Florence Vidor, Bebe Daniels, Pola Negri, and Clara Bow, among others.

Banton reached his peak in the thirties. Some of the most elegant and beautiful actresses in the world were under contract to Paramount then: Carole Lombard, Marlene Dietrich, Kay Francis, Lilyan Tashman, Claudette Colbert, Sylvia Sidney, Gail Patrick, and Texan Helen Vinson. When these stars were loaned to other studios to make films, they frequently demanded and got the services of Travis Banton. No designer in Hollywood was more highly regarded.

After fourteen years with Paramount, Banton left to open his own business. However, the studios exerted a strong pull, and the Texan worked for 20th Century-Fox from 1939 to 1941, then at Universal Studios from 1945 to 1948 as head stylist. Some of the most prestigious designers in Hollywood studied under Banton: Edith Head, Walter Plunkett, Gwen Wakeling, Jean Louis, and Vera West. His last film was *Valentino* in 1950.

World War I virtually shut down European film studios, and Hollywood attained the premier position of movie center of the world. Audiences flocked as never before to see their favorite stars, and films could hardly be made fast enough to satisfy the demand.

Gradually, the frenetic recruitment of directors became particular. Up until the war, almost any actor could take over the direction of a film. After the war, the director's job became increasingly demanding: first, because of the sophisticated methods developed by Griffith, and second, by the accelerating use of mobile cameras. Most of the earlier generation of directors had picked up their craft by watching Griffith or one of the other pioneer directors at work. After the war, filmmaking began to attract young men with a larger background — from a university or the professions, perhaps — with literary or intellectual interests that would serve them well when it came to making talking pictures.

Before 1914, the appeal of movies was specifically directed to the working class. Perilous and melodramatic subjects derived from the Victorian era: suffering heroines looking after orphaned brothers and sisters; sick or dying grandparents; handsome heroes; miraculous benefactors; villains. Then, at the threshold of the 1920s, a new middle-class audience appeared. Viewers now comprised prosperous working people and a conservative business element, which altered the social setting of contemporary film subjects. Lovely homes, gorgeous clothes, powerful cars, and the stimulating lives of an imaginary "leisure class" predominated. This became the desired but distorted image of the "normal" American's existence projected by the movies.

Thus the glamour age of Hollywood began, and with it began the careers of some of the loveliest stars on the screen.

☆
☆ ☆
☆ **2** ☆
☆ ☆
☆

The Glorious, Glamorous Years

The twenties was the Age of Idolatry. Aviators, baseball players, politicians, preachers and, above all, movie stars were the targets of this devotion. Silence was not a handicap on the screen. Rather, it tended to enhance the remoteness, the otherworldness of movie stars; to separate them from the commoners. It is significant that glamour in the twenties hinged, quite simply, on physical beauty.

The changing tastes and needs of the American public were reflected in the screen idols of the twenties; they were the fantasy projections of everyday life. Some of them promised new kinds of social or sexual experiences, while others reflected the more solid benefits of home and the familiar. Some offered dreams, others consolation.

Without doubt, the most enchanting stars created in the twenties were the flapper girls, as seen in Gloria Swanson, Colleen Moore, Clara Bow, and particularly the young Joan Crawford. They were pretty, tough, and knowledgeable, with inexhaustible resources of energy, spirit, and wit. They could dance until sunup, then Charleston all the way home. Without inhibition or embarrassment, they admired attractive men and pursued them unabashedly. But they were tough in order to protect their integrity, not to dispose of their purity. A man who got "fresh" might end up

22

with a sharp right to the chops. But if he was too reserved to make a pass, the flapper might get out of the car and walk home. Above all, the flapper personified *élan*.

The celebration of youth, beauty, and success was paramount in popular films of the day, and nobody conveyed the essence of the age more clearly and forcefully than Lucille LeSueur, alias Billie Cassin. She finally was called Joan Crawford, the name suggested by a fan in MGM's nationwide star-naming contest. Crawford despised the name because it reminded her of crawfish, a repulsive, pincered creature inhabiting the muddy Texas creeks that ran through the country where she was born.

It would be hard to imagine a life story more Dickensian than Joan Crawford's. When she was still a small child, her father deserted the family. Her mother then began a series of liaisons that sometimes ended in marriage. Whatever the case, existence for Lucille was measured out in daily doses of humiliation and rejection. Her mother forced the child to earn her way at school by scrubbing floors and waiting on the other students at table. The mother clearly preferred Lucille's older brother, Hal, to her. He stayed at home while Lucille was farmed out to the schools. Little Lucille hated and envied Hal at the same time. One doesn't have to be a psychiatrist to see personality complexes developing that haunted the adult Crawford's relationships with men and other women, and especially with her adopted children.

"What do you want more than anything in the world?" a companion asked Lucille LeSueur.

"Me?" said Lucille. "I want to be the most famous ballroom dancer in the world. I dream about it all the time."

Dancing had been the only activity in her adolescence that brought favorable comments from others. It is not surprising she saw it as a way out of her misery. When MGM executive Harry Rapf saw her dancing in the chorus line in a New York show, he was impressed with her looks and dancing skill. A note invited her to call on him at his hotel. She went. When Rapf offered her a contract, she was not especially impressed. Being a movie actress was not her dream, but the pay — $75 a week — was more than she or anyone in her family had ever earned.

A publicity man gave her a tour of the studio. On one stage she watched handsome Texan King Vidor directing matinee idol John Gilbert and D. W. Griffith's star Lillian Gish in *La Boheme*. She almost swooned. But her own screen test did not point to stardom. She could show emotion, but that was about it. Everything about her needed improvement, they said. So while the studio was "improving" her, she took to visiting all the sets to learn everything she could.

One day she struck up an acquaintance with Eleanor Boardman, who would become Mrs. King Vidor in the near future. She complained of the inactivity to Boardman. "Go see Harry Rapf," advised the star. "He's responsible for bringing you out here. Tell him you want to work — or else." Joan Crawford soon got small roles in several films, then appeared in *The Only Thing,* a screenplay starring Eleanor Boardman. The future Mrs. Vidor wanted to help.

Joan then became friends with gay actor William Haines. "Let me give you some advice," said the seasoned star. "You've got to draw attention to yourself. There are fifty other girls trying to get roles in pictures, and the producers don't know one pretty face from another. You've got to make yourself known."

To do that, Joan hit the nightclub circuit. Many evenings she brought home silver-plated trophy cups for being a superlative dancer of the Charleston. Naturally, producers in the popular clubs got to know her name, face, and style. And if she returned the cups the next day, as she frequently did to augment her income, management gave her $15 for each cup.

Fellow MGM player Marion Davies had William Randolph Hearst, and Norma Shearer had Irving Thalberg, but Joan Crawford had no patron. She had made friends, though, and she took the advice of one, a cameraman: she lost twenty pounds, and the effects were dramatic. The magnificent bone structure of her face became visible, and her figure improved perceptibly.

Joan learned her craft from fellow actors and from journeyman directors such as Edward Sedgwick, from Galveston. She took the advice of people she trusted, and she got lots of attention. Her screen persona was already forming. A group of movie advertisers named her a "Wampus Baby" of 1926, along with Texan Mary Brian and Texas-educated Dolores del Rio, who had been brought to Hollywood by Edwin Carewe. Making that illustrious list hardly guaranteed stardom, but many so-named actresses did make it to the top.

Crawford became friends with Dorothy Manners, another Texan, who served as assistant to Louella Parsons for thirty years before officially taking over Louella's column. "Joan was the queen," observed Manners, "and we were her ladies-in-waiting. She put on a show wherever she went. At a wedding, she was the bride. At a funeral, she was the corpse."

And the younger set gathered at Joan's favorite table at the Coconut Grove for dancing. Given a half-decent partner, Joan monopolized the dance floor. She dated and danced with Tommy Lee, son of radio millionaire Don Lee, and Michael Cudahy, of the meat-packing Cudahys. She also was attended at the tea dances by Howard Hughes, John Wayne, and J. Paul Getty, but these men who would soon wield so much power were far too shy to ask the Jazz Baby to dance.

Mike Cudahy was the first significant love of Crawford's Hollywood life. He had what she wanted: position, looks, a pleasant personality. And he was a great dancer. But Mike Cudahy also had a serious drinking problem, and a mama who thought he could do better than a Hollywood starlet named Joan Crawford.

In spite of a generally positive outlook, the aspiring actress became distressed over her lack of progress at MGM. Gish, Shearer, Boardman, Greta Garbo, and Marion Davies got important roles while she played in programmers (inexpensive films usually made with less than top-drawer talent). She began stopping at St. Augustine's Catholic Church across Washington Boulevard each morning to pray for stardom and love.

Desperate, she confronted Irving Thalberg, asking him why his wife (Norma Shearer) got all the choice roles. He urged her to be patient, claiming she still had much to learn. One of the things she had to learn was studio etiquette. By going directly to Thalberg, she breached it, and subsequently was thrown into a Western starring Tim McCoy, ironically called *The Law of the Range*. She would not allow herself to think of the role as punishment. Although uncomfortable around horses, she forced herself to overcome the fear, and she became one of the gang.

Thalberg rewarded her by putting her next into a movie with John Gilbert, then a huge star. Following that film, in 1928 she got her best role to date — an extension of her own personality — in *Our Dancing Daughters*. For the first time she was not merely the female interest of William Haines or John Gilbert. She was the star.

Louis Mayer recognized her worth by raising her salary to $500 a week, twice what it had been. Her St. Augustine prayers had been answered in the first part; now the second half remained. But that beneficence was just around the corner. He sported one of the ten most famous names in the world, with Jr. tacked on. More people recognized his father than photographs of Pope Pius XI, the King of England, Thomas Edison, or G. B. Shaw. Although he was several years younger than she, Douglas Fairbanks, Jr., was Joan's entree into Hollywood royalty. No one held more sway than the senior Fairbanks and his wife, Mary Pickford, the acknowledged king and queen of Hollywood.

Joan and Douglas Fairbanks, Jr., were married June 3, 1929, at St. Malachy's Church in New York, and moved into Joan's house at 426 North Bristol Avenue in Brentwood. The easy part was over. It would be tougher getting past the portals of Pickfair, and when she did, the air was chillingly forbidding. Doug Sr. took Jr. to play golf; Mary went upstairs to take a nap. Joan was left downstairs to knit, embroider, or hook rugs. Mary suspected that was not the only hooking her daughter-in-law had been up to. It was many months before the Fairbankses gave Joan anything like a welcome into the family. By that time, some of the luster had worn off Crawford's marriage, and she no longer coveted her in-laws' approval, except as a way of keeping score. She *was* the daughter-in-law of Hollywood's royalty, and by extension, royalty herself.

Following the great success of *Broadway Melody*, starring Bessie Love from Midland, Thalberg followed up with *Hollywoood Revue of 1929*. The film featured most of the stars on MGM's roster. Joan sang "I've Got a Feeling for You" and tap-danced before a male quintet. She also joined in "Singing in the Rain," the finale. Crawford proved a sensation in sound in theaters. She had cleared the hurdle that caused others to stumble.

Joan's success continued unabated in 1930. The next year, First National paid Douglas Fairbanks, Jr., $72,791, while Joan got $145,750 from MGM. She was worth twice as much as her husband, a situation that many couples cannot tolerate for very long. In the only way that really counts in Hollywood, she was more regnant than her husband.

In *Dance, Fools, Dance,* Crawford starred with Clark Gable in his second role of an MGM contract. The next picture he made with her was the most important to date in her professional career, *Possessed*. It ended her period in movies of playing the empty-headed hedonist who was obsessed with dance. She moved into portrayals of upwardly mobile girls who were on the rise from the lower classes. Her roles were an apt metaphor for America during the Depression. The movie roles also paralleled Crawford's struggle up from poverty.

Gable and his first wife, Josephine, had drifted apart. His new sponsor was a wealthy Houston widow, Maria Franklin Prentis Lucas Langham, eleven years his senior. He married Langham in 1931 and took on her three children from previous marriages as his stepchildren.

Joan Crawford and Gable had much in common personally by way of backgrounds, and she fell irresistibly in love with him. They became lovers and remained so as long as Gable lived, when they both were between marriages, or about to be, and sometimes during.

But Crawford was also much taken by Greta Garbo and followed her around secretly to watch her in action. One day Garbo saw her and took Joan's face in her hand.

"What a pity! Our first picture together and we don't work with each other. I am so sorry. You have a marvelous face," observed the Swede.

Recalling the incident much later, Joan said, "If there was ever a time in my life when I might have become a lesbian, that was it."

She must have meant an out-of-the-closet lesbian, for Crawford engaged in lesbian affairs throughout much of her adult life. Daughter Christina remembered an incident with a former nurse, who told her about Joan coming to her room after she had been drinking and inviting the woman to come to bed with her. The nurse refused, and Joan finally went away. The nurse kept her door locked after that, but Joan would get drunk and come pounding on it, begging her to unlock the door. The nurse finally could take it no longer and left the Crawford employ.

Reporting on Crawford after she had left MGM for Warner Brothers, Charles Higham wrote, "For years she had repressed her lesbianism while tormenting her immediate family with a kind of twisted rage. She had fought against her nature because she knew that even an inkling that this sainted Witch of the West had feet of clay might have caused her downfall."

According to Higham in his biography of Bette Davis, Crawford fostered a secret letch for Davis. Immediately after arriving at

Warner's in Burbank, she began sending Davis gifts and begging her to come to dinner. No one tried harder, says Higham, to seduce a beautiful woman than did Joan Crawford try with Bette Davis. Alas, it was to no avail. There probably was never a stronger professional rivalry between players than that between Davis and Crawford. But Crawford typically despised women and men who rejected her advances. It was thus a major surprise to insiders when the two actresses agreed to star in *Whatever Happened to Baby Jane?* Nothing came of it to further Crawford's yen for Davis, however. Davis, appearing on a TV talk show to publicize the movie, referred to herself and Crawford as "two old hags." Crawford immediately sent her a typed note on her personal stationery: "Dear Miss Davis: Please don't refer to me again as 'an old hag.' Sincerely, Joan Crawford."

Crawford had been allowed out of her contract at MGM by L. B. Mayer because he felt her appeal had run its course. She spent eighteen years at the Culver City studio — an exceptionally long time, even for an entire career. But Crawford knew it wasn't over. What she needed was a change, and the right role. She waited out the first two years of her Warner's contract until the script for *Mildred Pierce* was submitted for her approval. Her sense of material was still superb, and she won the Academy Award in 1946 for Best Actress, proving to all the nay-sayers that Joan Crawford was still queen.

If Hollywood loves anything more than a fall from grace, it is a sensational comeback. Yet it was the beginning of the end for her career. When it was clear her day had passed, she made a successful business career for herself through her marriage to the chief executive of Pepsi-Cola. She continued as a representative of that company, even after the death of Alfred Steele, her husband.

Crawford took up drinking alcohol at thirty-five. She quickly developed alcoholism, which she managed to control well enough to continue her career. She also was a smoker. And a Christian Scientist. About eighteen months before she died, she quit both alcohol and tobacco, finding them inconsistent with her religious beliefs. Anyone who has tried to quit either habit knows that it takes more than a passing whim to accomplish such a feat. She did both.

When Texan pal Dorothy Manners visited her in New York toward the end of her life, Joan fixed them a Texas breakfast of *hue-*

vos rancheros. "You know," she told Manners, "only a couple of old Texas broads could eat a breakfast like this."

Joan Crawford was tough. Longtime friend Adela Rogers St. Johns summed up Crawford's life not long after she died: "Joan Crawford was one girl Hollywood could never lick. Once or twice she lost a round, was down for a count of nine, had to outwait bad breaks. But overall Joan was never defeated by anything or anybody. She died last year a winner and still champion."

The transformation of little Lucille LeSueur from a San Antonio girl nobody wanted to Joan Crawford, movie star and business executive, has to be one of Hollywood's best examples of the Cinderella story.

During the thirties, the basis of glamour shifted from beauty to wit. In December 1933 the new glamour doll was appearing at Radio City Music Hall in a film called *Flying Down to Rio.* The billed stars were Dolores del Rio and Gene Raymond, but the town talked about the new dance team — lightfooted Fred Astaire and bubbly Ginger Rogers. Ginger's appeal was that she appeared to be a spectacular version of the girl next door, quick with a wisecrack, and decent — the kind of woman a guy would like to marry. She also possessed a cinematic quality that went beyond beauty, talent, or even precise analysis. Moviegoers spotted it instantly.

But Ginger Rogers was a girl of many faces, many talents, many characteristics. Although most moviegoers remember her as the pert blonde dancing the Carioca and any number of other dances, she was just as believable as a brunette or redhead, and the hair color change brought another dimension to her performance. She stated on numerous occasions the need to be flexible, a "chameleon of many colors." But she gave the impression that any hard-working and ambitious woman could achieve a success like hers, and that any man could find a captivating woman like Ginger for his wife. Lela Rogers, her mother, always tried to give the same impression to Ginger's friends, male or female. It was simply a matter of hard work and being ready when the break came.

What did Ginger Rogers represent in her heyday? An original? A caricature or a goddess? Or perhaps a smidgen of each? Like most major stars, she walked the fine line between originality and universality that is discoverable in artists since the beginning of time. She unquestionably received substantial support from her mother to get the big breaks and to sustain her career. But at what price glory? One marriage after another tumbled on the rocks below the precipice. While she always listened attentively to her mother for career and many other important decisions, she picked the men in her life herself. And all have been disasters.

Ginger was born, officially, in 1911, but longtime friends claim the year was 1908, in July. She, her mother, and father moved to Ennis, Texas, from Kansas City before she was a year old. The parents' marriage was shaky and failed soon after the move to Texas. The father kidnapped Ginger not once, but twice. Finally, Lela had a private detective track her down and she recovered Ginger. After that, the father saw little of Ginger during the last eight years of his life that remained.

Lela led an interesting life after her divorce. She went to Hollywood as a writer, won a short-story contest, and joined the Marines as one of the first women to do so. Ginger stayed with Lela's mother during this formative period of her life. When Lela left the Marines at the end of World War I, she resumed a romance with a man named John Rogers. They married in 1919 and moved to Dallas, where John was engaged in the insurance business. Ginger could see the beginnings of a perfect homelife with her mother and new father. The family moved to Fort Worth not long afterwards, and Ginger would later say that this is where life began for her.

A friend from those days, cartoonist Charles Cartwright, remembers Ginger well. But he doesn't claim to have spotted the latent talent that manifested itself a few years later. "She was attractive, with a great personality and boundless enthusiasm and energy, but as far as we were concerned, she was just 'one of the Cooper Street gang' " who wore out the rugs dancing the Charleston.

Ginger's early theatrical experience was limited to pageants written by her mother for local fund-raising events. In one, "The Birth of Music," which traced song and dance up to the 1920s, Ginger played Jazz Dancing, or Evil, and neighbor Florine McKinney was Classical Dancing, or Good.

When the Interstate Vaudeville Circuit announced a series of Charleston contests in several Texas cities, Ginger asserted her determination to enter them. Lela opposed the idea, fearing she would be charged with rigging the contests should Ginger win, since she wrote for a Fort Worth paper that publicized the events. Besides, much as she wanted her daughter to have a show business career, she wanted her to finish her education first. The gangly, freckled-faced youngster enlisted the aid of friends who finally prevailed upon Lela to let the girl enter. Lela sat up all night sewing a costume for her daughter to wear.

After Ginger won the Fort Worth contest held at the Majestic Theater, as determined by popular applause, she went to the state finals held at the Baker Hotel in Dallas in early December. The "Fort Worth Flash" was determined the "feet-up, hands-down" winner over 100 other contestants, and her reward was a four-week contract at $100 per on the Interstate Circuit, which included Texas, Alabama, and Arkansas.

"Winning that contest was without too much doubt the happiest day in my life," she said in 1936, after two marriages, major roles on Broadway, and several films with Fred Astaire.

Lela quit her job to organize Ginger's act. The young dancer played on every circuit she could find for the next two years. On the tour she ran into a dancer she had known in Texas by the name of Jack Culpepper. They fell madly in love during a three-week layoff and married in New Orleans in 1928. They became known professionally as Ginger and Pepper. Neither the act nor their marriage lasted a year. But Ginger showed her mother she was her own woman when it came to selecting men.

She went back on the road as a single act, then landed roles on Broadway, which led to Hollywood. Her first major chance came in *42nd Street*, a Warner Brothers musical. By 1933, musicals had surfeited American audiences, but Daryl Zanuck commissioned the new one to be special, and it was. Ginger played wisecracking Anytime Annie. The only time she said "no" was when she didn't understand the question. When the film opened in 1933, Louella Parsons praised Ruby Keeler and Dick Powell, but said of Ginger: "This isn't a one-woman or one-man production. Ginger Rogers is excellent as the affected chorus girl."

At the party after the premiere, Ginger excited gossips by arriving with young millionaire Howard Hughes, with whom she had an on-again, off-again romance during the next few years. Since nothing in the way of an offer ever came from Hughes, she married Lew Ayres. When that marriage cooled, once again her name was linked with Hughes. The association would have been attractive for practically any ambitious actress, or non-actress, for that matter. As a single woman and a top star, Rogers freely exercised her prerogative of carrying on romances with young men about town such as Jimmy Stewart, Cary Grant, Burgess Meredith, and others.

During her relationship with Hughes, he, typically, showered her with gifts, one of which was a new station wagon. After their affair ended, she went out to her garage one morning to find the car missing. After reporting the "theft" to police, she was chagrined to find afterward that the auto had always been registered to the Hughes Tool Company. Someone had merely picked up the wagon for them.

Noah Dietrich, former top Hughes executive, said in his autobiography that Ginger caught Hughes in bed with another girl and she cut him out of her life, once and for all.

Although Ginger Rogers is usually associated in the public mind with Fred Astaire, she won her Academy Award as Best Actress for a straight dramatic role. *Kitty Foyle,* based on a best-selling novel by Christopher Morley, tells about a white-collar girl's business life and love affairs. It proved to be a huge commercial success, as well as an Oscar-winning role for Ginger. Her competition that year was not lightweight: Katharine Hepburn, Bette Davis, Susan Hayward, and heavily favored Joan Fontaine. But on March 1, 1941, Ginger got the nod.

As Ginger's star rose, she did not always appear to her colleagues the way she did to moviegoers. She developed a reputation for being less than warm, for being calculating. She admitted to changes in her personal life. "I was trying to accomplish something, and you can't accomplish things without changing. That's the first rule of progress, isn't it?"

Her slide from superstardom began in 1944 with *Lady in the Dark.* The film grossed well, but it damaged her reputation. Her salary of $292,149 that year made her the industry's highest paid star, and she ranked behind only General Motors Chairman Charles E. Wilson as the eighth highest paid individual in the United States. Yet, her films continued the downward spiral, and as fewer offers came in, she considered campaigning for a congressional seat on the Republican ticket.

In 1948 Ginger had no films in release. She searched short stories, plays, novels, and scripts for the role that would propel her comeback, but none came. She kept physically active, read *Health and the Scriptures,* and kept a positive attitude. When Ginger heard that MGM was planning to follow up the highly successful *Easter Parade* with another Fred Astaire-Judy Garland original, she wrote producer Arthur Freed a letter congratulating him. Freed believed, correctly, that Ginger was reminding him of her own availability. Judy Garland's emotional and physical health were a known concern to Freed and his unit.

It was a shrewd, clever move on Ginger's part. Two days before production on *The Barkleys of Broadway* was to begin, Garland's doctor informed MGM executives that she had suffered an emotional collapse and would require at least three months to recover. Freed sent Ginger a script at her Portland, Oregon, ranch on Saturday, and she was at MGM the following Monday for costume fittings. She got $125,000 for her performance, and she was tickled to be working again. So were 5,000 of her fans who wrote the first week she was in front of the camera. The film was MGM's fifth top moneymaker of the year.

At the same time, Ginger and her third husband began drifting apart. In one of the little ironies prevalent in the stories of Texans in Hollywood, six months to the day after Port Arthur native Evelyn Keyes, then married to John Huston, introduced Ginger to Jacques Bergerac, Ginger married him. When that marriage ended, Bergerac became the husband of Dallasite star Dorothy Malone, before moving on to greener pastures.

By 1954, Ginger had accepted so many unsuitable parts merely to keep working that as lenient a critic as Dorothy Manners complained, "The veteran actress is far from her best in the new British production *[Twist of Fate]*." Even in television work, which she had entered in 1951, though far less demanding than theatrical films, she was let down. "Miss Rogers is a beautiful, slim, ageless woman who danced divinely. We watched her a hundred times in the darkness of the temples of youth. We remember her in slapstick comedy and heavy drama full of sin and suffering and too many sequins. On TV, she is naturally welcomed as an old friend, but she never reaches us as Mr. Bolger does." Another critic got to the point: "Ginger and Ray appear in a merely so-so show."

Rogers stayed out of films between 1957 and 1964. Although she appeared in a few TV variety shows, most of her time was spent polishing rusty stage technique in stock. Determined to survive, she began a tour in surefire *Annie Get Your Gun*. Her performance received an enthusiastic review from Elliot Norton: "Miss Rogers has to force her voice to fill the Carousel, which is almost as big as Fenway Park. The important point is that she does it. You get the strong and exhilarating feeling that there is nothing she wants to do on stage that she can't or won't do. She has the skill, the force, the personal charm and the terrific sense of professionalism — which involves obligation to an audience — that are irresistible." She kept touring.

David Merrick chose her as the replacement for Carol Channing in *Hello, Dolly*, after a run of 652 performances. She began working with a voice coach, and three months after her role as the mother in the film *Harlow*, she appeared as Dolly Levi at the St. James Theater on August 9, 1965. Fans gave her a standing ovation before she spoke a word. Some of the reviewers felt her performance less powerful than Channing's, but Ginger's fans loved her. She came out looking like a movie star every time.

After eighteen months on Broadway, Ginger took a vacation before joining the national company of the show. The group was made up of players from the Mary Martin and Betty Grable troupes. While on the tour, Rogers visited a hospital filled with veterans. A triple amputee who had not responded to hospital treatment of any kind reached up with his one arm and pulled Ginger close. An aide attempted to extricate her, but Ginger signaled she wanted to be left with the patient. She stood there for forty-five minutes talking to the boy. He was crying. Ginger was crying. So was the female aide. From that time on, the young man responded to treatment.

On the strength of Ginger's superstardom, nostalgic appeal, and success in *Hello, Dolly*, she got a startling contract: $12,000 a week for fifty-four weeks to headline *Mame*. It was the largest figure ever paid an actor in the history of London's legitimate theater.

At the end of the London run, she was hired to be a representative of J.C. Penney's. Everywhere she went across the country, women turned out in masses. In 1972 Penney's expanded her role as a representative because, said Ginger, "I'm Mrs. America. Ladies identify with this American apple-pie face." Just as they had in the thirties, when everyone was forty years younger.

Since 1972, Ginger Rogers has continued to perform in stage work, and fans have remained faithful to this survivor, who now spends time in Dallas when she is not working, or Fort Worth, where it all began.

Mary Martin, sometimes called the "Weatherford Whiz," was a friend of Ginger Rogers and Florine McKinney. Florine lived two houses down from Ginger in Fort Worth on Cooper Street. Mary Martin achieved unique distinction by becoming a member of the "Cooper Street Gang," the only outsider to be so honored. She was allowed in because she could dance a mean Charleston. Not as well as Rogers, of course.

McKinney was the prettiest of the three girls, but despite Lela Rogers's help in getting her movie career under way, she had the least success. Mary Martin didn't set the woods on fire either, at first. She taught dance at her own studio in Weatherford before heading to Hollywood. It was quite a while before someone suggested she try Broadway. Naturally, as soon as she proved herself in New York, Hollywood crooked its finger, and she arrived as a star. But after making nearly a dozen movies, Martin never found the work congenial. She achieved her greatest fame on the stage. And as Larry Hagman's mother.

While attending a party in New York not long after she first arrived, Martin was introduced by producer Richard Kollmar to the star of *Knickerbocker Holiday*. Walter Huston threw her into a fit of amazement by kissing her on the cheek. Then he said, "I probably am the only person in New York City who knows where Weatherford, Texas, is. I even know which water pipes go to your house." Then he explained.

Huston was trying desperately to get his acting career going in the early days of the century. During a tour, he met pretty Rhea Gore, a girl with Texas roots. They fell in love and married. When son John was born in 1906, Walter knew he had to get a job that paid regularly. He had had college training in engineering, so he took a job with the Weatherford Public Works Department to support his family. Thus, he knew the particulars of Martin's pipes.

"People are starved for glamour, because there is so much dullness in their everyday lives," once said Ann Miller. "They look to stars to provide it, off screen as well as on. That's why this wave of nostalgia has swept the country — because the thirties, forties and early fifties were a glamour era.''

Ann Miller ought to know, having provided the country with glamour for over fifty years. In 1986 she was still tapping away on stage in *Sugar Babies,* with Mickey Rooney her co-star. Together they set new records with the show.

Similar to other actresses from an earlier era, a controversy exists regarding Miller's age. She says she was born in 1923; a birth certificate says 1919. It would seem of little consequence today, but as she says, "four years can mean a lot to a girl."

Miller, like Crawford and Rogers, achieved film fame through her dancing skills. And like Mary Martin, she had to go to Broadway from Hollywood before Hollywood would accept her as a star. Accept her they did, however. And as she acquired cinematic prestige, she acquired masculine admirers of mogul rank.

Louis B. Mayer had fallen hard for Jean Howard, a glamorous actress from Dallas, a few years before his glance fell on Miller. He was seeing Howard while still encumbered with Mrs. Mayer, but he was trying to work out an accommodation of all three. To place things in proper perspective, he arranged passage for himself, Mrs. Mayer, and Miss Howard on the same ship going to Europe. When it became apparent that Howard was otherwise occupied with a Hollywood lawyer-agent on the trip and would not be subject to the mogul's calls, Mayer was reduced to tears. She told him she thought he merely wanted to show her Europe, that he expected nothing more from her than filial appreciation. Besides, she explained, she and agent Charles Feldman (known in Hollywood as "the Jewish Clark Gable") could not keep their hands off each other. They were in love.

Mayer responded: "Since Feldman can't keep his hands off you, let him pay your bills." When he got back to Hollywood several weeks later, Mayer barred Feldman from the MGM lot. "Don't ever let that son-of-a-bitch through the gates again," he instructed his security chief. "Unless I need him."

When little Annie Miller entered Mayer's life, he experienced *déjà vu.* . . . something about Texas women. He begged and pleaded, according to Miller's account of the affair. But her mother would not let her marry him, despite the fact that by this time he had dumped Mrs. Mayer after forty-odd years of marriage. Mayer finally found another woman to wed, but he reportedly was not happy with her. Perhaps she was from the wrong state.

Miller eventually did marry, against her mother's wishes. And, says Miller, "all of my three husbands had quite a lot in common. Texas is oil country, and maybe subconsciously that's why I was attracted to men who made their living in oil. All three were oillionaires. Two were Texas oil men. The other was from an old pioneer California family. All of my husbands were handsome, rich, and utterly charming when they were sober. They were all basically playboys and quite spoiled. All my husbands wanted to be married bachelors, and I was too dumb to catch on."

Her first real acting role came in *Stage Door* with Ginger Rogers, Katharine Hepburn, Adolphe Menjou, and Lucille Ball. "I think the only reason I was considered in the first place was that Lucille Ball put in a good word for me and she was Ginger's dearest friend," recalls Miller. In addition to the good role, *Stage Door* was important to Miller because it introduced her to Ginger Rogers, Ann's childhood idol, "who has remained a good friend to this day."

When Hollywood roles became scarce for the dancer at the end of the thirties, she took a part in *George White's Scandals of 1939*. Miller turned out, to the surprise of many, to be the new smash hit of the show. She was given credit by critics for keeping the show on Broadway for a year, and then another year on tour. Damon Runyon, writing for the *New York Daily Mirror*, noted that "All the talented and beautiful young ladies are coming from Texas lately. Miss Mary Martin, who is certainly one, if not the other, is from there. So is Miss Ann Miller, who is both. . . . She can dance almost any other young lady dancer in the business right out of the theatre."

Ann Miller lived at the Gorman, a hotel popular then with show people in New York. Mary Martin had the penthouse right above Miller and her mother just before Martin returned to Hollywood a star. They became good friends.

When Miller left Hollywood for Broadway, she earned $250 a week. When she returned to Hollywood, she received $3,000. One of the first films she made was a million-dollar singing Western starring Gene Autry called *Melody Ranch*. He had asked for her, and she brags about giving him his first screen kiss. After that movie, she called herself the "Queen of the Bees." And in truth, the "B" movies were her home for a long time afterward.

At about this time, Linda Darnell and Miller did a lot of double-dating. Ann's agent, Vic Orsatti, was madly in love with Linda, and Ann was frequently escorted by wealthy, society playboy types. Among her dates: Al Bloomingdale, of Bloomingdales; Jerry Orbach, of Orbach's department stores; and Harry Karl, of Karl's shoe stores. Karl later latched onto El Pasoan Debbie Reynolds after the Eddie Fisher-Liz Taylor romance turned into divorce for the singer and Reynolds. Ann Miller even dated Howard Hughes. Once.

"Let me make it clear," said Miller emphatically, "I was *not* one of Howard's 'girls' or girl friends. He only asked me for the one date on behalf of his girl friend of the moment, my friend, Linda Darnell." Hughes supposedly was madly in love with Linda, but the relationship was troubled with a problem that he thought Ann could help with.

All the glamour women from Texas in the thirties and forties kept close relationships with each other. Besides Linda Darnell, who was a bridesmaid at two of Miller's weddings, Miller was good friends with Ann Sheridan from Denton. And Ann Sheridan was good friends with everybody.

She was known as "a good guy" when that was a complimentary phrase for a woman. Sheridan had a quick wit, a very pretty face above a so-so figure, and an ability to drink, cuss, and joke with the cream of the masculine crop. And they all respected her. She was a drinking buddy of Jimmy Cagney and Humphrey Bogart and Errol Flynn. She married actor Edward Norris in 1936. In exactly 375 days, she was a widow at the age of twenty-two. Next, she married one of Bette Davis's old flames, actor George Brent. That lasted only 263 days. Why? "Brent bent," she told an acquaintance in front of a reliable witness.

She did not believe a hex was on her marital chances, but the male relationship that lasted longest was with publicity agent Steve Hannigan. He died a bachelor after eight years with Ann. He also left her $200,000 in his will. Nevertheless, Sheridan married again, the last time to actor Scott McKay. It was not a memorable liaison, lasting only seven months. This time, she was the one who died.

Ann Sheridan, dubbed the "Oomph Girl," was one of the very few beauty contest winners who forged a film career from that launching pad. Yet, she could have been successful whatever her line of endeavor. She and Jack Warner were frequently at swords' point, and she frequently "struck," i.e., she was placed on suspension for not accepting whatever role Warner offered her. Ann Sheridan knew what she wanted and refused to accept trash as film vehicles.

During World War II, her face, along with Linda Darnell's, were favorites with GIs all over the world. The films of both were moneymakers, if not always highly artistic successes. It would have been impossible for a contemporary man in his mid-twenties, say, gazing at their vibrant, celluloid images, to realize the two beauties would die tragically.

Ann Sheridan died a few days before her fifty-second birthday, of cancer. Darnell, a victim of alcoholism, fell asleep watching one of her old movies on television at the home of her former secretary. A drink in one hand, cigarette in the other. There was no way she could have gotten out of the fire, given her blood-alcohol level at the time of death. Linda Darnell was dead at the age of forty-four.

The pitiful demise of many who trekked to Hollywood proved that all that glittered was not gold in the glamour era. It was especially true of a Houstonite named Howard Hughes.

3

The Last Tycoon

Thirty minutes from Houston, his old hometown, he died at 3,000 feet in the air. His death attracted front-page headlines around the world, but he received none of the public eulogies usually accorded wealthy, famous, powerful figures. A loved one remaining behind said, "I'm saddened." And that is all ex-wife Jean Peters would say. There were few mourners for the enigma that had been Howard Hughes.

He had lived the American Dream, was in fact a folk hero, "perhaps the single most representative American of the twentieth century," according to one biographer. But not one public figure stepped forward to praise the man or his deeds. Not one of his Hollywood associates, aviation confreres, nor politicians that he supported acknowledged his passing. Howard Hughes had become a pariah.

Hughes was still a teenager when he headed west to Eden to chase his passions: films, airplanes, and women. In Hollywood, Howard set about learning how to make films with the same ardor that he designed and raced airplanes and pursued women and wealth and power.

In 1930 Grauman's Chinese Theatre premiered the most expensive film ever made at that time, *Hell's Angels*. (Even today it is listed by *Motion Picture Almanac* as one of the top 100 films ever made.) Airplanes suspended along Hollywood Boulevard were caught in searchlights blazoning the arrival of the long-awaited film marvel. All the stars came out to the first public showing. Fans screamed from the bleachers and had to be restrained by police when their favorites stepped from limousines.

Sid Grauman, owner of the Chinese Theatre, was a power in Hollywood, and a film he chose to premiere there had commercial greatness stamped on it. When Grauman went to New York for the Big Apple premiere of *Angels,* he grabbed all the publicity Howard Hughes expected for himself as the writer, producer, and director of the film. Howard promptly knocked Grauman down with a sharp right to the jaw. Who did Sid think he was dealing with?

Hughes proved he wasn't a Johnny One Note by following up *Hell's Angels* with a string of big hits and minor classics: *The Front Page, Scarface,* and *The Outlaw.* With *Scarface* he had his first run-in with the Hays Office, a censorship bureau set up by the Hollywood moguls to keep movies clean enough to prevent government intervention and boycotts by religious groups. Hughes reshot extensively, attempting to satisfy Hays, but he still did not get approval. The Texas outlaw decided to release the uncut version. He wasn't in debt to the censorship bureau. What could they do to him?

The Hollywood Reporter, an independent voice in the movie industry, backed Hughes publicly. The daily publication called the film "a masterpiece of acting, directing, and producing," and offered kudos to Hughes for making a film that exposed the mobs and their gangland operations. The movie, of course, became a film classic, and it did much to enhance Hughes's Hollywood reputation as a filmmaker.

For *The Outlaw,* filmed in 1939, Hughes featured a new starlet, nineteen-year-old Jane Russell. Jack Buetel played the male lead as Billy the Kid. King Vidor had directed a major film of the outlaw's life in 1930, but that didn't deter Hughes. He wanted to do something different: he was going to make it sexier than any Western had ever been. Up to that time, all Westerns had been rather sexless.

Jack Buetel was only twenty-three at the time and had recently arrived from his birthplace, Dallas. His only experience had been in little theater and some radio. Hughes liked him, his baby face, his handsomeness, and put him under contract.

Hughes was something of an outlaw himself with this picture. The Breen Office told Hughes in advance the script would not receive a seal of approval, but the Texan went ahead anyway. Making the film proved at least as difficult as *Hell's Angels,* perhaps more so. Production occupied more than a year of Hughes's time. No movie had been completed before under circumstances as difficult as this company encountered.

When the Breen Office told Hughes they would not give the seal of approval without changes, he sued Motion Picture Association of America, the office in charge of the Breen bureau. He produced evidence to show that female breasts had been a prominent part of many earlier movies. On March 23, 1941, the seal of approval finally was granted.

After a two-year publicity campaign, Hughes released the film for only ten weeks, then withdrew it. In 1946 he re-released it, even though the Breen Office tried to take away its seal. Also, the Catholic Legion of Decency objected to its release. No critic in this country or Britain liked it; they thought it a trashy film. But it made millions in profits, and provided reams of publicity for Hughes. He was already becoming a legend as a producer — and as a playboy.

Always on his arm was an endless succession of screen goddesses, some of whom he created himself. Platinum Blonde Jean Harlow was an extra until Hughes starred her in *Hell's Angels;* Jane Russell, the Buxom Bombshell, had just stopped being a high school student when Hughes signed her and put her most prominent features forward in *The Outlaw.* But if Hughes was known for the women he kept, he was also known to keep separate his business and pleasure. Harlow said the closest he came to making a pass at her was asking if she would like a bite of his cookie.

Howard Hughes had the most unusual career of any Texan who ever went to Hollywood. He was young, rich, tall, and handsome; he was also shy, awkward, and uncomfortable around others. He had the same appetites as other men, plus perhaps a few others, and he was able to indulge them to the fullest. But he kept remarkable control of himself until that July day in 1946 when he crashed his experimental airplane into the Beverly Hills home of actress Rosemary de Camp. His chest was crushed, one lung collapsed, seven ribs were broken, his head severely lacerated, and he was cut and burned all over. After that, Howard Hughes was never the same. Doctors gave him only a few hours to live, so they administered morphine copiously to relieve the excruciating pain. But the tough Texan persisted in living; indeed, within a month after his discharge from the hospital he was flying again. But the long, slow spiral into drug addiction and madness had begun.

During the spring of 1922, Howard Hughes's beautiful, thirty-nine-year-old mother entered Baptist Hospital for simple surgery on her uterus. She died from the anesthetic. Hughes's father was too shattered by her death to tell his son what had happened. That task fell to Uncle Rupert Hughes, the literary lion and Hollywood screenwriter. Less than two years later, the senior Hughes underwent a convulsion and died from a heart attack. Neither mother nor father had shown any signs of ill health.

Part of the family fortune was spread among Hughes relatives. Howard was only eighteen when his father died, and as a minor, he could not sign contracts. He went to court, and upon reaching the age of nineteen was declared legally independent under Texas law. He bought out the relatives, including Uncle Rupert, in order to be in complete charge of the family businesses.

Howard married Ella Rice in June 1925, six months short of his twentieth birthday. They left Houston in September on a train for Los Angeles. Howard intended to become a film producer. Hollywood was a thriving community at the time, and Hughes quickly became known as "the sucker with the dough." It took a while for Hollywood to discover that this shy, gangling youth had a spine of iron.

For his first effort, Hughes hired an actor — sometime writer, sometime director, and a family friend from Houston — named Ralph Graves. Because he had been a film business associate of his father, Howard thought it would be all right to put him in charge. The movie that resulted, called *Swell Hogan,* cost $40,000 and was so bad it was never released. Howard Hughes didn't look back.

Everybody's Acting was the next production. But Hughes was smarter this time; he hired veteran director Mickey Neilan to construct the outline of the movie. Neilan had also known Howard's father, but he did not have to rely on family contacts; he had made two dozen or so films since 1919 and had a sound reputation as a film director. The film was a success and earned enough profits to cover the losses on *Swell Hogan.*

Next Hughes formed the Caddo film company, which he named after his Louisiana oil operation. He then contracted with established director Lewis Milestone for Caddo's first production, *Two Arabian Nights*. This film was successful, too, a knockabout comedy somewhat similar to *What Price Glory?*. Milestone's direction was superb, and Hughes's money provided solid production values to the film. Good reviews and public acceptance followed.

On May 16, 1929, when the first Academy Awards were given in the Blossom Room of the Hotel Roosevelt, the director's award for comedy went to Milestone. Frank Borzage also won for his drama, *Seventh Heaven*. This was the first and only time two separate awards were given for directorial achievement.

When *Two Arabian Nights* was released in October 1927, Howard was still only twenty-one years old. He must have felt vindicated in his decision to enter filmmaking. Rupert Hughes had tried to discourage Howard after the *Swell Hogan* disaster, but that event merely provided a challenge to Howard. "I had to prove me right and them wrong," he said.

Howard Hughes's method for teaching himself to make movies is revealed by an incident that happened with Milestone on *Arabian Nights*. The director could tell the kind of man he was dealing with early on, so he had it written into his contract with Hughes that he, Milestone, had final cutting rights. After he had finished the movie and before its release, Milestone went on a vacation that took him out of town. One of Milestone's spies called and told him Howard was recutting his film. Milestone rushed back to Hollywood and confronted Hughes, who sat hunched over a Moviola, the editing machine.

"Relax," said Howard. "Your film has already been shipped. I made a copy and I'm just taking it apart to see how you put it together."

"Hollywood was Howard's classroom," recalled Lewis Milestone. "He was learning about movies. He was the type of person who could never accept anything as the truth unless he had learned it or experienced it personally for himself. He would not take anyone's word for it. He had to do it, and store it away in that genius mind of his."

As soon as *Nights* was completed, Hughes started preproduction work on *Hell's Angels*. It was Hughes's dream project. He was a great admirer of World War I fighter pilots, and in *Angels* he was able to exercise that interest. He received his own pilot's license on January 7, 1928, three months after starting preparations for his aviation film. It was typical of Hughes that he became qualified to do whatever it was he filmed.

In the meantime, Milestone directed another Hughes film, *The Racket,* in the summer of 1928. It was the first of a series of gangster films that became a staple during the thirties. Three months later, Hughes released *The Mating Call,* directed by highly rated James Cruze. The film was thought to be pretty racy material for 1928, with scenes of sexual passion and frustration. The movie was a hit and cleaned up at the box office. Howard Hughes was, as they say, on a roll.

He had hired Mickey Neilan to develop the outline for *Angels,* and scriptwriter Harry Behn to turn out the script from it. Hughes had been impressed with Behn's work on King Vidor's massive hit of 1925, *The Big Parade,* a war movie that ran two years on Broadway and grossed the equivalent of $35 million in 1985 currency.

Hell's Angels started out a silent film, starring Bebe Daniels's husband Ben Lyon, Texan James Hall, and a foreign female star. When Hughes decided to reshoot the film as a talkie, the foreign actress could not pass vocal muster and had to be replaced. Hughes considered Ann Harding, the beautiful blonde star who was born in San Antonio. He finally concluded she was too genteel and sophisticated, both as an actress and as a person. That was not the part. It was more of a Jean Harlow part, Hughes decided, and it made a star of her. But Hughes showed no personal interest in the Platinum Blonde. "As far as I'm concerned," she said, "I might be another airplane. He expects you to work the same way. Never get tired, give your best performance at any hour of the day, never think about anything else."

Despite the great success of *Hell's Angels,* Hughes maintained an air of modesty which shocked Hollywood. The rule there was, "he who tooteth not his own horn, goeth untooted." Hughes admitted he had learned a lot, but he credited those who worked for him with the film's success. The role he played as co-writer-producer-director, he said, was his biggest error. The film would have been finished sooner and cost less if he had not tried to do everything himself. "I had to worry about money, sign checks, hire pilots, get planes, cast everything, direct the whole thing. Trying to do the work of 12 men was just dumbness on my part. I learned by bitter experience that no one man can know everything."

Hughes's single-minded devotion to whatever interested him at the moment led to wife Ella suing for divorce. He never had time for her nor any interest in her affairs. As soon as she returned to Houston to file, he started going out publicly, accompanying an amazingly long line of beautiful movie stars. Ella became the belle of the ball in Houston with the $2 million her husband settled on her.

Hughes supposedly fell in love with many of the women he saw, but his courtship always followed the same pattern he established with Ella. Initially, he showed tremendous interest and devotion to the woman, but when he got her, he lost interest and went back to his solitary agenda.

Wilson Heller, one of Hollywood's earliest publicists and Howard Hughes's first press agent, recalled: "He had some wealthy dame from Chicago, who was living up in Montecito, right outside Santa Barbara. Every time he got a new plane, we would fly up there. He would zoom down over her house, trying to attract her attention. A few times, he came damn near to hitting her chimney. He could scare you to death. Howard was a very good pilot, but he was a daredevil. . . . He was a brave man. I never knew a braver person than Hughes, and I'd flown in combat with the best.

"He could do so many things at the same time. But whatever else he did, he was always on the make for women. From what I heard, he was the world's worst guy in the hay. Two of his girlfriends told me he wasn't worth a damn as a lover. He was just no good in the sack. They said he just wanted to look and fondle."

Heller had gone to work for Hughes when Howard was hip deep in production of *Hell's Angels*. Heller already had a long list of stars for whom he served as press agent, and he wasn't eager to chuck all that to work for Hughes. He was never sure that Hughes might not just take off somewhere with a new woman.

One of the first stars Hughes had become enamored of was the beautiful Billie Dove. He put her under the surveillance of a private investigator, as he was to do with other women he dated. He wanted to know who they saw, when, where, and so on. He also obtained medical records for each woman, a manifestation of his fear that he might catch a germ or disease from one of them.

When Billie Dove's husband, Irvin Willat, discovered

Hughes's interest in his wife, he refused to give her a divorce unless Hughes laid a goodly sum on him — $325,000, to be precise. Hughes wanted her so badly he willingly paid Willat for a quiet divorce. That payoff set a pattern for Hughes and his women.

In the meantime, Lewis Milestone had one more film to do for Hughes, *The Front Page*. It was the story of *Chicago Examiner* editor Walter Howey, and it provided the model for all future newspaper movies. Mary Brian, a luscious beauty from Corsicana, played the female lead, while Adolphe Menjou portrayed the character modeled on Howey. *The Front Page* turned out to be a winner with the critics and the public.

The next bead on Hughes's necklace of successes was *Scarface*, starring Paul Muni, in 1932. The movie won high praise, once again, from all the critics, and the public went to see it in droves. It was the gangster picture to end all gangster pictures.

Then Howard Hughes did something entirely unexpected, unreasonable, and illogical. He quit pictures for aviation. It was the middle of 1932, and he was twenty-six years old.

Many young men had taken on Hollywood and failed, but Howard Hughes had tried and succeeded. He had made eleven movies, three of which were enormously successful and which became minor classics. No one before or since has quit at such a point. But that was only par for Howard Hughes. Success in films was like a beautiful woman he had wooed and won; he was no longer interested in her after she succumbed to his seduction.

But Hughes's social life during the thirties included many famous actresses: Katharine Hepburn, whom he loved madly, and who finally rejected him without damaging his ego. Bette Davis, who, despite her iron-woman image, was gentle with Hughes when he suffered from ejaculatory impotence and would have married him if her husband had not blackmailed Hughes. And Ginger Rogers, with whom he carried on a romance extending over several years, until she caught him in bed with another woman.

Hepburn received an old-fashioned romantic overture from Howard. He flew over her house, dipping his wings in salute; he even taught her to fly. When Hepburn went on tour with a stage production of *Jane Eyre* during severe winter weather, Hughes tagged along at a safe distance in one of his airplanes. He laid a new emerald next to her hairbrush on the dressing room table each night before she went onstage. With Hepburn, Hughes had met someone who coveted privacy as much as he did. Yet the more they tried to avoid it, the more publicity they attracted. Katie eventually had to let him go. Reluctantly, but firmly.

Hughes was not as attentive to Bette Davis as Hepburn, but in one respect he actually was closer to Davis. She did not possess Hepburn's beauty, and somehow that reduced Howard's anxiety, enabling him to perform sexually. Davis did not threaten him; she was sweet and kind, and that helped him overcome his impotence.

Davis, of course, had more to do in life than cure impotent males. She was still enmeshed in a thorny relationship with director William Wyler, as well as a moribund marriage. Her husband, a man named Ham Nelson, was driven wild by her infatuation with Wyler and then Hughes. Ham decided to bug their house in Coldwater Canyon, obtaining the help of a confederate who placed the bugs then laid lines out to a truck where they were hooked to a recording device.

One night Ham, whipped into a fury by what he heard going on in his bedroom, raced to the house and into the room where Hughes was being ministered to by Davis. Howard, tangled in the sheets, tried desperately to punch Ham in the face, but he was unsuccessful.

Nelson vowed to wreck his wife's career with the recordings, and the year being 1939 he could have done it. But after reasoning with the outraged husband, Hughes finally persuaded Ham to give up the recordings by agreeing to pay him $70,000. Hughes could scarcely abide having his potency problem made known to his friends, thus destroying his macho image. He hired a professional killer to do away with Nelson. Just in time, he learned that Ham had told the police Hughes would be responsible should anything happen to him. Howard immediately sent a check by messenger to Nelson, who smashed the vinyl recordings before Bette's eyes. Naturally, the comic-nightmare episode ended her fling with Hughes, as her husband hoped it would. Davis then took out a loan against her salary to pay Hughes back, a matter of great honor to her. Hughes, wealthy as Croesus, did not refuse the payment. He did, however, send her a solitary flower each and every year on the anniversary of the repayment for as long as he lived.

Hughes carried on romantic attachments with various actresses throughout the forties and fifties, until he married Jean Peters. They had been companions for years until Peters finally decided nothing would come of it and married wealthy Stuart Cramer, who had oil interests in Texas. When Hughes found out that she had married him, he put a stop to the union. Within a few days, Peters separated from Cramer and soon filed for divorce. She finally married Hughes in 1957.

In one of the curious quirks of living and loving in Hollywood, Cramer turned around and married actress Terry Moore in 1959. They had two children. Moore had earlier been married to West Point football star Glenn Davis, but she swore in court after Hughes's death that she had been and was still married to Hughes when he died. She told *Playboy* magazine that the Hughes estate gave her enough to live comfortably, on the interest alone, for the rest of her life.

According to a man named Johnny Meyer, Hughes also had interests in men. Meyer had worked for years as a pimp and henchman for Errol Flynn before going to work for Hughes. He was accustomed to fulfilling the whims of his employers, and nothing shocked him. Meyer recalled, before his mysterious death in 1978, that "Howard Hughes . . . was in my opinion, and I was as close to him as anyone, definitely bisexual. That whole image of his, of having women stashed away in apartments that were set up for him, was a lot of baloney. In fact, I deliberately set up these women as a disguise for him. In most cases, he never even went to bed with them. He could go by and discuss the latest events and disappear, in the confident knowledge that the press was following to the front door and would report on the period he had spent there, imagining all kinds of macho events going on inside.

"The fact of the matter is that I doubt if Howard went to bed with these girls more than once or twice. . . . I don't think he could satisfy women and I very much doubt if he ever had an orgasm with one. On the other hand, he was fascinated by men. In complete secrecy, I would arrange assignations for him with boy hustlers. At one time, in a spirit of outrageousness, I actually set him up on a date with Errol."

Meyer described the meeting that took place late at night in Santa Barbara, far from Hollywood. Errol Flynn showed up in a new Packard, looking very drunk; Howard drove his battered old Chevy. He rolled up the windows, looking to right and left, terrified he might be seen. Then he crept into the house with Flynn, hat pulled over his face, wearing a Bogart trenchcoat. Meyer took off, fearing law enforcement officials might be waiting for the two men. "I have no idea whether they went to bed or not. But I think it is likely," said Meyer.

His last days were spent in a self-made prison. He was a naked old man in horrible pain and ultimate terror. One hundred twenty pounds of flesh stretched over his six-foot, four-inch frame. No color was detectable, not even in his lips. Long gray hair reached midpoint of his back, and his scraggly beard fell nearly to his navel. His chest sunk nearly to his backbone, and hideous nails extended several inches from the tips of his fingers, amber spirals that seemed to be the only signs of life coming from the body. His teeth, not brushed in years, were rotting stumps that looked like blackened tree trunks after a forest fire. A tumor had grown from the side of his head. Finally, one of his shoulder blades — bare bone — poked through his paper-thin skin. Needle tracks marched up and down both arms and thighs. A horrible cluster centered around his groin.

Many addicts have wondered what it would be like to have all the money they needed to support their habit. This is it. Howard Hughes was a billionaire junkie.

Sometimes he would "double-pump" a hit, shooting the drugs into his veins, then pulling the plunger back with his blood into the syringe, then shooting it back into his system. He would lie back and relax in the first rush of relief. Sometimes a jingle would escape his lips, a little scat lyric he remembered from the old days: "Hey-bop-a-ree bop. Hey-bop-a-ree-bop." Sometimes he even chuckled to himself.

The effects of fame and fortune are somewhat exaggerated in the case of Howard Hughes, but similar stories ran rampant in early Hollywood. Soon, the corrupt lives of the stars began seeping into subjects for the big screen.

Dope and sex scandals of the early twenties had forced the moguls to hire Will Hays, an upstanding Presbyterian and former Cabinet member, to head the agency that policed movies and those who made them. Morals clauses became a part of every actor's contract. What the Hays Office did was force aberrant, or rather embarrassing, behavior to go underground. As long as it stayed off the front pages of newspapers, the moguls were content. They did the same things as their stars, but they knew how to protect themselves.

When the Depression came, after the first surge of enthusiasm for the talkies, theater attendance dropped precipitously. Not only were people broke, many preferred the free entertainment provided by radio in their own homes. To whip up interest, moviemakers turned increasingly to violence and sex in their product. Conditions got so bad by 1934 that Catholic bishops forced a new production code on the industry. They threatened to forbid Catholics to attend movies not approved by the Church, and film studios could not tolerate that loss. The studios acceded to the wishes of the Legion of Decency.

And the era of the singing cowboy began.

4

Singing in the Saddle

The Western had been a staple of Hollywood fare since *The Great Train Robbery* in 1903, but the genre became stale and needed something to jazz it up. Musicals had been extremely popular when sound movies started — indeed, they saved the day for some studios before audiences became surfeited.

Then an idea popped up to combine cowboys and music. It had never been done before. Producers tried it out with Ken Maynard first, a cowboy holdover from the old, silent days. They even gave newcomer John Wayne a shot at it, but his singing had to be dubbed — besides, it seemed kind of sissy to him.

What the movies needed was a clean-cut, clean-living actor, untainted by scandal, who could ride a horse, stand up for right and justice, and sing a little.

What they needed was Gene Autry.

Born on a ranch near Tioga in North Texas seven years into the twentieth century, Gene Autry had spent enough time working cattle and fixing fences in hot Texas and Oklahoma summers to know he didn't care for it a lot. He was working as a telegrapher for the railroad in Sapulpa, Oklahoma, when Will Rogers heard him singing to his own guitar accompaniment and offered him encouragement to pursue a career in entertainment.

After a while he took Rogers's advice and went to New York to try his luck. He was told to go back home and get more experience, preferably on radio. Autry did just that, landing a nonpaying job on Tulsa's KVOO. He got exposure and considerably improved his musical technique. After several months, as his popularity increased, record companies sought him out. Victor invited him to New York to make a recording.

"I cut a recording for Victor," Autry remembers. "I've forgotten what it was. Johnny Marvin, a friend of mine from Oklahoma who was a top recording artist for Victor at the time, and his brother, Frankie, played with me for the recording." Autry was to talk later with the Victor artist and repertory director, Loren Watson.

Arthur Satherley, in the meantime, had just gone to work for American Record Corporation. He advised Gene to go ahead and talk with Watson, but not to sign with Victor until he, Satherley, talked with him.

"I'm just starting out here with American Record and if you'll sign with me," Satherley told him, "I'll do everything in the world I can to promote you. You'd be my first artist. Victor is a big company and they have several big artists that they have to concentrate on. I don't think you'll get the promotion from Victor that I can give you."

After Autry thought it over, he decided Satherley was right and signed with American Record Corporation. The company produced records under various labels for sale through numerous chain stores, and it featured Gene on the Okeh label. Sears Roebuck was his major outlet.

The first song he recorded, "That Silver-Haired Daddy of Mine," one he co-wrote with Jimmie Davis, his former boss in Oklahoma, sold 30,000 copies the first month, 300,000 during the first burst of popularity (in 1930), and eventually millions were sold.

Sears representatives, to put it mildly, were ecstatic. They figured the cowboy singer could sell clothing and appliances as well as songs. Soon they put him on their Chicago station, WLS (World's Largest Store), in his own show, "The Gene Autry Program," at the handsome sum of $35 a week. Autry eventually appeared on WLS's "National Barn Dance," one of the earliest country and western radio programs in the country. The producer of Chicago's Barn Dance was George Hay, who went to Nashville four or five years later and started the Grand Ole Opry. He liked Gene and took him on tours with other Barn Dance performers.

The sandy-haired Texan was also a big hit in public appearances and came to the attention of Herbert J. Yates, owner of American Record Corporation and, by 1935, Republic Pictures. Yates put Autry under contract and sent him to Hollywood under a picture contract in 1934, much to the singer's delight, along with his radio sidekick, Smiley Burnette. Gene was paid $100 a week and Burnette, $75. Autry's first part was in Ken Maynard's *In Old Santa Fe*. He sang a couple of songs and attracted more favorable attention. Although his part was small, he overshadowed Maynard, then in declining popularity. Fans wrote in, complaining that Gene didn't get to do enough in the film, and they demanded more.

Autry played supporting roles in two serials before starring in *Tumbling Tumbleweeds* in 1935. His apprenticeship status as an actor was quite clear to critics at this time, and they complained that he sounded "as if he had just come from elocution class." The words were clear and precise but carried little meaning or emphasis. It made little difference to fans: *Tumbling Tumbleweeds* received a highly enthusiastic welcome by moviegoers in rural America who paid their dimes and quarters for an hour's respite from the grind of the Great Depression.

Autry said later, after he had achieved certified national appeal, "I know I'm no great actor, and I'm not a great rider, and I'm not a great singer; but what the hell is my opinion when fifty million people think I'm pretty good?"

With *Tumbling Tumbleweeds*, the formula for the next fifty Gene Autry films was established. The singing cowboy (Gene) riding the World's Wonder Horse (Champion) with a comic sidekick (Smiley Burnette) encountered evil characters attempting to do good people out of something. Sometimes the pretty leading lady was innocently involved with the black hats and worked against Gene, but truth won out and she fell for the good-looking cowpoke before the final reel.

Gene found reasons to break into five to eight songs per film, usually at a hoedown or radio broadcast. But if the plot didn't provide a logical excuse for song, that didn't stop the cowboy from providing one. In *The Singing Cowboys*, David Rothel cites a classic example in *Mexicali Rose*. Gene, captured and tied up by Mexican *banditos*, learns the leader is a fan of Gene Autry records. (Autry performed under his own name in all his starring films — the first actor ever to do so.) The gang has carried a small, portable windup phonograph and records from camp to camp, and when the leader's favorite record gets broken, Gene breaks into the title song with full orchestral accompaniment, in the middle of the desert.

Such anomalies never fazed Gene's fans at all; in fact, they loved the fantastic aspects of their hero's exploits. Gene Autry placed first in the *Motion Picture Herald* poll of top moneymaking Western stars from 1937 through 1942, when he joined the Army Air Corps. He also sold a lot of cowboy records.

Despite success in both media, making eight popular films in 1936 and also 1937, each of which grossed at least three times the cost of production, Gene Autry was paid only $150 a week — $50 more than his starting salary as an untested player in 1934. The arrangement was inequitable, and the star complained. Herbert Yates, penny-pinching head of Republic, tried to negotiate with Gene, but the talks broke down. Autry had discovered his films were being used as leaders in block booking, whereby exhibitors could rent his films only by taking a huge block of Republic's inferior (and cheaply produced) movies. The singing cowboy heartily disapproved of the practice *and* his low salary, and walked out on Republic. He called his director at the time, Joe Kane. "Don't break your neck getting ready for the next picture, because I won't be there," Gene told him.

In an interview with Charles Flynn and Todd McCarthy (*King of the Bs*), Kane said, "They chased him all over the South — he was very big in the South. [Autry was on a personal appearance tour.] Process servers tried to catch him. He was so popular in these small towns, the people would just surround those process servers and gently walk them out of town. They never did catch him. . . . [Republic executives] didn't know it, but Autry had a nice nest egg. They thought he was broke. . . . Autry was never broke. . . . They finally had to settle with Autry because he wouldn't come back, except on his terms. They paid him what he wanted. . . ."

What he wanted was $12,500 per film at the rate of six to eight films per year. In addition to his picture salary and recording revenues, Gene made another $25,000 a year from the sale of Gene Autry-licensed paraphernalia associated with cowboying, such as cap pistols, holsters, spurs, and chaps. In early 1940 Gene began broadcasts from "Melody Ranch" for Doublemint gum, for which he received $1,500 for each thirty-minute weekly episode. His radio salary eventually reached $5,000 per week.

In the autumn of 1939, Autry's fan mail clocked in at the rate of 50,000 pieces per month, which exceeded by 1,000 the previous record set by Clara Bow. He was the top Western star in 1940 and ranked fourth on the list of *all* Hollywood moneymaking stars the same year. Only Mickey Rooney, Spencer Tracy, and Clark Gable outranked him.

Gene's movies never played first-run theaters, which makes this feat all the more impressive. Small towns provided the cowboy's base of loyal, devoted fans. Some of the towns were so small, said Gene at the time, that "even Mrs. Roosevelt hasn't been there." One Texas community had a population of 252, but boasted a theater seating 450. Folks traveled long distances over rutted roads to town to hear Gene warble and watch him fight the baddies.

But the Texan's appeal was not limited to the United States. In a 1939 tour through the British Isles, he was greeted by cheering crowds of fans. Five hundred thousand turned out to see him ride Champion in a parade down the streets of Dublin, and after sold-out performances at the city's Theatre Royal, enthusiasts filled the alley behind the theater. On Autry's last night, the alley was jammed. "I never heard anything like it. They sang 'Come Back to Erin,' and weaved back and forth," remembers the singer. "It was a very heart-touching scene."

In 1941 the 227 souls of the little community of Berwyn, Oklahoma, voted unanimously to rename their town Gene Autry. Gene told *Life* magazine then, "You could spend weeks and never find such a natural location for a movie."

After enlisting in the U.S. Army Air Corps and serving as a pilot ferrying troops and supplies in North Africa and the Far East, Gene returned to Hollywood to find that during his wartime absence his place as the leading singing cowboy in movies had been taken over by Roy Rogers. Although five years younger than Autry, Rogers had not been drafted due to the number of his dependent children.

Rogers's wife, Dale Evans, would soon become the Queen of the Westerns. After a progression from her home in Uvalde to marriage at fourteen, motherhood at fifteen, and widowhood at seventeen, Evans settled into the saddle alongside her husband.

Gene Autry returned to Republic in mid-1946, exactly four years from the time he left it. He was nearing forty years of age, a more mature and much wiser man than the one who volunteered for the Air Corps in July 1942. He had five pictures remaining on his contract with Republic, and he tried to negotiate a new deal with Yates that would allow him to produce his own films under the banner of Gene Autry Productions. Autry wanted more control over his own films, but mainly he was interested in not having to split profits on his own work. Autry was one of the first stars seeking this arrangement; by the late fifties, most big stars and directors had it. Thus, Gene was not only the pathfinder of a new film genre, he showed the way in film business dealings as well.

Tight-fisted Yates refused the cowboy's demands and Gene went to Columbia studio at the expiration of his contract in mid-1947. Columbia gave him a lucrative contract — in fact, everything that Yates refused.

Although Autry walked through the first four of the five films he owed Republic and received generally unfavorable reviews, his last, *Robin Hood of Texas*, was quite good. "This is right in the groove for Autry fans"; "He's the Autry of old, singing better than ever," said critics. Perhaps this was the Texan's way of thumbing his nose goodbye to the irascible Yates.

The films Autry made for Columbia (1947–1953) are some of the best B-Western films made, though they were overshadowed by Roy Rogers's flashier ones. However, by 1947, national magazines started writing features about Gene's big, diverse businesses. *Life* titled one article "Gene Autry, Inc.," and *Time* labeled one of theirs "Cowboy in Clover." His holdings included his own film company, radio stations, a radio production company, oil wells in Texas and New Mexico, cattle ranches in Arizona, Nevada, and Texas, two newspapers in Phoenix, a $2-million traveling rodeo, majority stock position in a book-publishing firm that put out Gene Autry comic books, five movie theaters in Dallas, music publishing companies, a California-based flying school and charter service, a grocery store in Oklahoma City, and the licensing of products bearing his name worth $100,000 a year by 1947. In 1948, Autry's net income surpassed the half-million mark.

In the films made at Columbia, Autry introduced subtle but

noticeable alterations. He soon got away from the flashy, flamboyant costumes of the thirties and early forties, the kind that country and western singers Porter Waggoner and Hank Snow were famous for, and substituted plain denim outfits. Unless, of course, demands of the plot — a social occasion, for example — called for dressing up. Gene also performed fewer songs and focused more on rough-and-tumble action, much to the delight of his fans.

In Gene's earlier Columbia features, Pat Buttram filled the role of sidekick until he was seriously injured. A cannon blew up and ripped open his chest. Champion received a severe cut on his nose from the shrapnel, but miraculously, Gene Autry didn't get a scratch, although he was in the scene being filmed. His former sidekick, Smiley Burnette, was also under contract to Columbia, but he appeared in Charles Starrett films. As if to put a final period to the movie careers that began together, Smiley finished his Starrett commitment in time to appear with pal Gene in Autry's last six films. The final one, *The Last of the Pony Riders,* was completed in 1953.

Gene Autry was the last of the veteran singing cowboys to perform in theatrical films, and he had appeared in more films than any other star in the genre — ninety-one.

At the time Gene went to Columbia for film work, he also agreed to release his records on the Columbia label and become a top recording artist for it with songs such as "Mule Train," "Buttons and Bows," and "Ghost Riders in the Sky." In addition, seasonal favorites "Here Comes Peter Cottontail" and "Frosty the Snowman" became big hits, as well as the most popular Autry record of all, "Rudolph the Red Nosed Reindeer," a song he disliked intensely. The singing cowboy sold over 49 million records during the course of his active performing career, and the holiday songs still enjoy good sales.

As Autry's film career wound down, his television interests geared up. His "Flying A Productions" was responsible for eighty-five "Gene Autry Show" half-hour films between 1950 and 1954, and seventy-six half-hour "Range Rider" films beginning in 1951, starring Jock Mahoney and Texan Dick Jones. In 1952 his company produced the first thirty-nine episodes of "Death Valley Days," followed by eighty "Annie Oakley" half-hour films starting in 1953. Two years later, Flying A Productions began its last two series, "Buffalo Bill, Jr.," with forty-six half-hour films starring

Dick Jones again, and twenty-six half-hour films starring Gene's horse, Champion.

The advent of commercial television was viewed by the motion picture industry as the devil incarnate. After a federal court anti-trust ruling in 1948 divested film studios of their theater holdings and broke up the illegal practice of block bookings, and after the storm produced by the postwar Communist witchhunt in Hollywood, television was seen as the third event in a group of catastrophes that seems to affect show business in trios.

The premier show business "outlaw," Gene Autry was the first movie star to appear on television. "Well, I caught all kinds of hell from theater owners, exhibitors, and even from Columbia Pictures [Gene's movie releasing company]. They were all over me for making this first series."

At a convention of the Theater Owners of America at about the same time, Autry addressed the assemblage in no uncertain terms, telling them they had feared radio when it first came in and now they feared television and tried to pretend it didn't exist. (In fact, film studios had steadfastly refused to photograph TV sets in living room scenes until the late fifties, and movie star contracts forbade actors to appear on television, even for interviews.) He told the producers in the crowd that they would all be making movies for television before long and would end up selling their old product to the new entertainment medium.

The singing cowboy was on the cutting edge of the entertainment conglomerate. His television series went into reruns in 1954, and his radio broadcasts from "Melody Ranch" ceased two years later. The metamorphosis of Gene Autry from cowboy performer to cowboy tycoon was complete.

When *Newsweek* magazine reported early in the sixties that Autry had purchased his fifth hotel, and that he was seeking FCC approval to operate KTLA-TV in Los Angeles, Gene said he was only trying to "build a secure future."

With Robert Lehman (of Wall Street's Lehman Brothers) and Harvey Firestone, the Texan owned majority stock positions in: Golden West Broadcasting — radio stations located in major West Coast cities — worth $17 million; the California Angels baseball team — $8 million; and the Gene Autry Hotel Company — $18 million. In addition to these investments, Gene still owned the properties mentioned earlier, plus television stations in Phoenix and

Tucson, and had a minority stock position in the Los Angeles Rams football team.

In time, Gene Autry developed a mystique typical of Texans in general, and specifically of current Texan entertainers-businessmen like Willie Nelson. He is the dichotomy of a shy, good-ole-boy cowboy performer and a cunning, shrewd businessman who, it is claimed, has amassed a fortune of over $100 million, making him one of the wealthiest individuals in the United States.

Ted Rogers, an Autry business associate, concludes that "Gene is one of the most socially shy guys I've ever met that made it big as a public figure. He is just terribly shy. So you can imagine how uncomfortable he is around, say, Eastern establishment people or advertising networks, pseudosophisticated, wheeling-dealing kinds of people — lawyers and accountants." According to Rogers, Gene was a slow business study, but a thorough one who took full personal responsibility for all the decisions he made.

Nevertheless, Gene Autry made excellent moves that propelled him to the forefront of the entertainment business and to a leading role in a variety of business enterprises. He doesn't do much at all to promote himself in a public way, but privately he holds a handful of aces.

And not one breath of scandal has ever touched his private or public life. As the Tioga Texan celebrated his eightieth birthday, there was still much to learn about one of the Lone Star State's favorite sons.

After Gene Autry showed them how to do it, all the studios rustled up their own singing cowboys. Most of them were not sensational, although some were far better singers than the Texan. Autry, however, had a charisma lacking in the others that appealed to rural audiences. And by the mid-thirties, half the movie theaters in the country were located in communities of 5,000 population or less.

The feared and hated radio networks were raided for talent, particularly the ones playing country music. An independent Hollywood producer, Edward Finney, picked the co-host of the WHN Barn Dance that originated in New York to star in a series of Westerns for Grand National — a Poverty Row studio. The new star was Woodward Maurice Ritter.

Born in Panola County in East Texas, Ritter spent most of his early life in Nederland, near Beaumont. He came under the influence of J. Frank Dobie at The University of Texas and studied folklore and western history before pursuing law studies at Northwestern University. Then he set out for New York in 1929, determined to carve out a career on Broadway. He appeared in five productions, including *Green Grow the Lilacs.*

On October 31, 1932, he made his first recording for American Record Company, Gene Autry's old label. Ritter also appeared on two radio shows, where he picked up the nickname "Tex."

Ritter was perfect for the part Finney had in mind. "I listened to some of the records he had made for Decca," said the producer, and they "were exactly what I had in mind." Also, Ritter really was from Texas, and his rough voice expressed authority and authenticity not found among other singing cowboys. Further, although he never gained great stature as an actor, he read his lines far better than other Western film stars. Ritter had a rhythm, a sense of the language and meaning that other performers lacked. His ultimate fame rests in country music, but in 1936 he set out to acquire filmic acclaim, and he got it almost immediately.

Ritter's first film, *Song of the Gringo,* was released in November 1936, and the second only one month later. During the next nine years, he completed almost five dozen movies for Grand National, Monogram, Columbia, Universal, and PRC. The last was *Flaming Bullets* in 1945.

Unquestionably, Tex Ritter's career as an actor was immensely enhanced by the success of his recordings. After lackluster years with Decca (1935–1939), he switched to Capitol in 1942 and produced many hits, especially during the war years. However, it was in 1952 that Ritter gained international recognition as a singer, and that for a movie title song.

Gary Cooper starred in a film called *High Noon* that year. During its filming, the star was an ill man in tremendous pain much of the time, and it showed on film. Upon its completion, the director was not satisfied with the way the story came together in the cutting room. He and his film editor worked and reworked the footage with some success, but an ingredient was still lacking to make the story a success. The director then had Dmitri Tiompkin, the musical director of the film, write special theme music; Ned Washington wrote the lyrics to it. They got the most original Texas singer of that time to record it, and the rest is film history.

Since musicals were first presented on stage, producers have wanted theatergoers to leave humming the tunes. The same wish holds true for film producers. Singable lyrics or hummable tunes will not make a bad picture good, but it is hard to overestimate the impact of a good theme song on the popularity of a movie.

The songs of cowboy films harked back to a romantic West that had great appeal to rural audiences who wanted escape from the realities of Depression and then war years. Tex Ritter provided a voice they could trust. He exhibited a genuineness not found in better singers who donned Western clothes and sang of roundups they knew nothing about. Ritter possessed that honest sincerity of all good country-western singers, and he was not ashamed to be one. Rural audiences recognized his unalloyed validity and responded to it.

Bob Wills was another musician born in East Texas — Kosse, in Limestone County — in 1905. He grew up picking cotton alongside black field hands, listening to their music as they sang the blues of their tough life. It was tough for white Bob Wills and his family, too, and they traveled northwest through Fort Worth to their final destination of Turkey when Bob was a youngster.

The family continued picking cotton, but they also played ranch parties on the weekends. Bob made his first "professional" appearance at the age of ten, playing his fiddle. Attempts to earn a living as a barber were not greatly successful, and Bob turned again to his music for a living. Locked up for drunkenness in his hometown of Turkey, disgraced in his own eyes, Wills headed for Fort Worth and eventual fame as a bandleader.

After several years of playing in and around Fort Worth, Wills broke with his radio sponsor, Burrus Mills, and its representative, W. Lee O'Daniel. He spent a short time in Waco before heading for Oklahoma. O'Daniel (later governor of Texas) filed a lawsuit against Wills, which O'Daniel lost, but he continued to hound Wills for leaving Burrus Mills and wanted to drive him out of the music business altogether. Threatened economic reprisal cost the Bob Wills band a job on a radio station in Oklahoma City, but Wills told the manager of KVOO in Tulsa all the details of his difficulties with O'Daniel. The manager hired the Texas band anyway. O'Daniel tried to get Wills fired once again, but this time the threat didn't work, and Wills went on to considerable fame broadcasting over KVOO. He also sold a lot of flour for his sponsor.

When Gene Autry left Republic in 1937, he made a rural tour of Texas, Oklahoma, New Mexico, and Louisiana. Bob Wills was on that tour. He and Autry were close friends, and Autry spread the word about Wills in Hollywood. The singer was offered a start in films before, but did not accept until 1940. Monogram offered him second lead in support of Tex Ritter in *Take Me Back to Oklahoma*, and the King of Western Swing signed a contract. At the time, Bob Wills and his Texas Playboys were riding a wave of success with "San Antonio Rose." When the movie played in Tulsa, Wills was given precedence over Ritter in the film credits.

Response to the Wills band, smaller than usual in the film, was strong, and he next made *Go West Young Lady* for Columbia the following year. As a consequence of this film, Wills signed a pact to do eight more for Columbia, with Russell Hayden as the star. Wills's performances as an actor were somewhat stiff but acceptable. His music and reputation made him a valuable addition to the motion pictures in which he appeared.

Another Texas singer, Ernest Tubb, made his first film in 1941. He played in support of Charles Starrett in *Fightin' Buckaroo* and *Ridin' West* in 1942. A 1943 film, *Jamboree*, was the last one he made until the 1947 musical extravaganza called *Hollywood Barn Dance*. Tubb, while a popular and influential singer and stage performer, was not ideally suited to films. Physically he appeared gaunt, and Hollywood efforts to help him gain weight failed. Also, Ernest Tubb's persona simply could not be captured on film as it was experienced in person.

There were other Texas musicians who didn't particularly qualify as popular singing cowboys, but they did sing in Westerns. Smith Ballew's voice was dubbed in for John Wayne's in Wayne's brief foray into singing cowboy movies. The voice did not sound especially authentic, but Smith was a tall, rangy Texan in appearance, and studios thought that was all it took to be successful. Ballew had led a big band while in college and afterward, but he was not at home as a Western singer and performer.

Art Davis was a former Western swing fiddler with Bill Boyd's Cowboy Ramblers; he also played with Gene Autry's band. Davis appeared on screen in several singing roles, but he had the opposite problem of Ernest Tubb: he couldn't lose weight. Everybody thought he would make a fine lead player if he slimmed down. Alas, it was not to be.

Bill Boyd and Art Davis had recorded together as far back as 1934, and in 1942 they were reunited in six low-budget films for Producers Releasing Company, a Poverty Row outfit. All were released the same year they were completed. Neither man made any films of consequence after these. Boyd went back to Dallas, where he resumed a successful radio, record, and stage career. He died in Fort Worth in 1977.

One of the final Texas singing cowboys of this era was Eddie Dean Glosup, born in Posey in 1907. (He dropped his last name when he got to Hollywood.) Although he was typically scorned as a film actor, Dean had perhaps the finest voice of any of the singing cowboys in terms of pure, lyrical quality. As a songwriter, he produced at least two country classics, "One Has My Name (the Other Has My Heart)" and "I Dreamed of a Hillbilly Heaven," as well as a Western classic, "On the Banks of the Sunny San Juan." He had only three years as a singing cowboy, but the first year, 1946, he was among the top ten moneymakers of Western films. He followed with similar rankings in 1947 and 1948. During this period, Dean starred in twenty films for PRC and another Poverty Row company, Eagle-Lion.

Monte Hale, born in 1921 in San Angelo, became a professional singer by age twelve. In his early twenties, he was discovered while singing in a USO show and brought to Hollywood. By 1944 he appeared in *Stepping in Society* and *Big Bonanza*. He played in support of fellow Texan Sunset Carson at Republic until 1946, when he got his own starring musical series. Herbert J. Yates thought enough of Hale to shoot nearly half of his nineteen films in color. When the film series ended in 1949, he went back to singing on stage, but he was not notably successful in personal appearances or on records. His last two films were *Giant,* 1956, and *Guns of a Stranger,* 1973.

After the terrible realities of a world war and the frightening spectre of atomic attack, interest in singing Westerns, about a West that never was, diminished drastically. Also, the impact of television was quickly felt. Many of the vintage Westerns were edited for television, and Hollywood saw no need to produce more. The cycle of singing cowboy films slowed to a sad halt, a victim of changing public taste and the exciting new medium of free entertainment, television.

Tex Ritter's last film was in 1945, Eddie Dean's in 1948. Gene Autry, the man who started it all, quit, appropriately enough, with *Last of the Pony Riders* in 1953.

Gene Autry was not afraid of the new medium, however. He began his own half-hour series in 1951 and produced eighty-five programs by 1954. His company, Flying A Productions, provided many Western shows for television, and gave lots of work to Texas actors in the fifties.

The singing cowboys would not disappear forever. Their influence on Texans in Hollywood and elsewhere continues to this day, in a somewhat different fashion. Music and films seem inextricably bound, or perhaps we should say that music, films, and Texans are inextricably bound. A combination of Texas songwriters, singers, and actors erupted in the seventies and evolved into a powerful force in the eighties.

The leader of the pack is Willie Nelson, who appears to defy the law of gravity.

5

Our Heroes Are Still Cowboys

While a boy during the Depression in Abbott, Texas, Willie Nelson learned all the cowboy songs from Saturday serials and singing-cowboy Western movies.

"Those were my heroes when I was growing up," recalls Willie, "And I think every little kid I knew thought the greatest thing in the world would be to be in the movies."

In the forties, hearing the Texas Troubadour Ernest Tubb crank out songs on the Grand Ole Opry, in a voice once uncharitably described as "the screech of an owl with emphysema," Willie determined that he would become a singer. He had already become a songwriter at the tender age of seven by composing lyrics in the "cheatin'" motif. When he was ten he presented a folio of fifteen songs as a present to his mother. On the cover he had printed in a scrawl, "Songs by Willie Nelson."

"But when I first saw Gene Autry," he remembers, "there was no doubt in my mind that was what I wanted to be — a cowboy movie star."

In 1979, riding a tall wave of personal popularity as Country Music Association's Entertainer of the Year, Willie got his chance. He had attended a Nashville party in honor of Robert Redford thrown by recording producer Billy Sherrill. Redford was in town raising funds for environmentalist projects. When the party ended, he and Nelson happened to be on the same plane headed for California. After an hour of casual conversation, Redford asked Willie if he was interested in making movies. The singer admitted he was, that in fact he had been offered roles before but turned them down because, "I wasn't sure either one of us knew what we were doing."

Redford told him about his current involvement with *The Electric Horseman* project and told Willie there was a part for which he would be ideal, that of the ex-rodeo star's manager and friend. Some time passed, and eventually they made the movie. Redford played the hero, a parody of a real cowboy, who earned his living selling breakfast cereal in an electrically lighted, rhinestone-covered outfit.

Nelson received uniformly good notices for his work, and an ad-libbed line of his drew the biggest laugh in the movie. When asked by another character his plans for that evening, Willie, in character, responded, "I'm gonna get me a bottle of tequila, a Keno girl who can suck the chrome off a trailer hitch, and kinda kick back."

Of the part, Nelson said, "I just play myself . . . do all the lines and the reactions the way I would do them normally." A critic thought he was totally convincing, and fellow professional actors complimented him for his realistic portrayal. Sidney Pollack, who directed the singer in *Horseman,* says "he has a built-in sense of truth."

Willie had been told that it took honesty to be a good actor, and he understood. Because that is exactly what it took to be a good country songwriter and performer.

Although he had long wanted to turn the story of his *Red Headed Stranger* album into a movie, Willie's next movie project was the starring role in *Honeysuckle Rose,* scripted by fellow Austinite Bill Wittliff. It is essentially the story of Willie Nelson and hundreds of other country performers "on the road." When someone complained to director Jerry Schatzberg after a preview screening of the film that there was too much music, that it interfered with the story, he replied: "You must not have been listening to the music, because the music *is* the story." Schatzberg had told the story of love through the music.

Even Willie's young leading lady, Amy Irving, with whom his

character falls in love, did not understand the role of the music either.

"I didn't know it was going to be a concert film or I wouldn't have been interested in doing it," she said after the movie was released.

But that attitude came later. During the filming of *Honeysuckle Rose,* which took place mostly in and around Austin, "the open romance between aging Willie and his lovely co-star is an amazing real-life enactment of the movie's script," chirped a gossip columnist.

"Those newspapers are just looking for something to write about," answers Willie. "Amy and I, we became good friends. . . . The script called for some good old-fashioned romance, and I never thought it was illegal for people to enjoy working together. Amy Irving's a beautiful lady."

While shooting the scene at a gathering where Buck Bonham, the name of Willie's character, is to perform, lovely, blonde Dyan Cannon, playing Buck's wife, stepped on stage and announced she was divorcing him. The extras who made up the audience, mostly local people who adored Willie and knew that his real wife was also pretty and blonde, booed Cannon from the stage until they were convinced the scene was only make-believe.

Someone asked Willie how his family liked the movie. "Connie saw it, and . . . she likes it," he answered. "She likes the way the guy comes home to his wife in the end."

Nelson was accused by some Nashville pickers of "selling out" by working in films, criticism he quickly brushed aside: "Sounds like a lot of jealousy to me. I don't think there's a guitar player in the country who wouldn't go to Hollywood and make a movie, if he were asked. If there is, I'd like to meet him. He's an idiot."

Honeysuckle Rose was not a favorite film of the critics, and blame was shifted about from writer to director and back again. Some of it landed on Willie's shoulders too. But the soundtrack of the movie took off like a hound chasing a Texas jackrabbit, receiving more advance orders than any other Willie Nelson album to that time.

The album also silenced critics who felt Willie had lost his songwriting talent, since all the songs he recorded the previous three years were written by someone else. Jerry Schatzberg had told Willie on a plane flight from Georgia to Austin that if he didn't write some new songs for the film, he wouldn't have a chance at an

Academy Award for music. Willie whipped out a pencil and within five minutes had scribbled the lyrics to "On the Road Again" on the back of his plane ticket. The mouths of his director and producer dropped a foot or so. The song won a Grammy award for Best Country Song of 1980. Willie got an Oscar nomination for original soundtrack composer.

The singer-actor had a small, well-received part in James Caan's movie called *Thief* before he and Wittliff combined efforts again to make *Barbarosa.* Willie played the part of a middle-aged gunfighter whose ears have been cut off for stealing cattle. He marries into an aristocratic Mexican family, but they shun him, blaming him for corrupting the family blood. Three generations of the Mexican family try to kill him. All fail.

Fred Shepisi, a highly touted Australian filmmaker, directed the mythic Western. What he, Wittliff, and Nelson sought was a redefinition of the American Western, the movie genre that Willie and others of his generation loved so much. Willie and Wittliff wanted an "outsider" to interpret the script, one who could see beyond the surface of the cowboy-gunfighter story into its mythic qualities. The completed film did just that and achieved wide critical acclaim, if not box-office success. Critic Janet Maslin of *The New York Times* called it "the best western in a long while . . . *Barbarosa* . . . uses one American legend, Willie Nelson, to create another, and Mr. Nelson has more than enough grace, grandeur, and magnetism for the job." Another critic claimed Willie's "the best face since Humphrey Bogart."

Many offers of new film projects poured in. And Wittliff penned a script for *The Red Headed Stranger,* for which Willie wanted Robert Redford to star. The script was sold to Universal but nothing came of it, and the Austin team repurchased the screenplay.

Nelson next made a film called *Songwriter* with good friend Kris Kristofferson, a Texas cohort. The movie contains large chunks of autobiography and accurately represents the life led by country poets like Willie, Kris, and Waylon Jennings. Another Texan in the cast is serious actor Rip Torn, who turns in a sterling performance as the double-dealing manager of an Austin auditorium that books country-western acts. That temperamental Broadway and film star Torn would agree to be in the movie (he also appeared at about the same time with Kristofferson in another) gives some indication of the stature Willie Nelson films had achieved by that time.

In the meantime, Willie starred in a CBS television movie called *Coming Out of the Ice*, a story of two Americans imprisoned in Siberia. There were no traces of Willie the singer, but plenty of signs of Willie Nelson, accomplished actor.

After several jerky starts and stops, the script of *Red Headed Stranger* finally was filmed in 1985. Originally, it had a budget of $12 million when it was to be shot with Hollywood financial backing. But Willie saw control of the project slipping away to the men with the money, and he could not allow that to happen. By putting up much of the money himself, along with some from Darrell Royal, Bud Shrake and others, Willie Nelson maintained artistic control of the movie.

Working closely with Willie, Dallasite Morgan Fairchild, Katherine Ross, and some of Nelson's band members, plus lots of supporters from around Austin, Director Bill Wittliff brought the movie in one day under filming schedule and slightly under budget at $3.5 million.

In previous movies, Willie Nelson was concerned solely with acting and music. In *Stranger*, he co-produced and co-wrote with Wittliff, and starred in the film. He also had a say in editing, distribution, and promotion.

When the curtain fell at the conclusion of the premiere of *Red Headed Stranger* in February 1987, not many felt the movie was a success. It did not break any attendance records and quickly disappeared from the nation's screens.

What made it possible for a person with Willie Nelson's background to become a popular film star? Especially one who entered the film arena when most performers' eyes are turning toward retirement rather than to new fields to plow? It had a lot to do with the transition he experienced in the sixties and early seventies.

When the youth movement swept the country, Willie, though no longer a youngster himself, fit right in. He was disillusioned, disappointed, and disgusted with the Establishment. He had gone to Nashville with some of the best songs in the business, and he kept writing them. But they became hits for other singers. Within nine months in 1961, four of his songs reached country's Top 20.

"Crazy," recorded by Patsy Cline, and "Hello Walls," sung by Faron Young, even made the *pop* Top 20. In early 1962, Willie's own version of "Touch Me" made the country Top 10.

But it was a long time between drinks from the well of massive public acceptance for the Texan. None of his records reached the country Top 10 again until 1975, when his "Blue Eyes Cryin' In The Rain" from the *Red Headed Stranger* album did it for him.

Nashville was a conservative town when Willie plied his trade there in the sixties. The recording powers had a very narrow view of what themes were acceptable to country audiences and what clothes were taboo. Willie Nelson and Waylon Jennings, as well as a couple of others, believed honesty dictated a wider range in those two areas. They rebelled against the music establishment in Nashville and became so-called Outlaws. They grew beards and long hair, openly ignored drug laws, and wore "hippie" clothes.

Although Willie made a good living from his song royalties, he wasn't doing so well as a performer on records. Mainly because he couldn't make them in his own style. He pulled out of Nashville and went home to Texas.

Nelson changed record labels so he could have artistic control. "It was hard not to get discouraged and throw it all away at times," says the singer. "But I felt in the back of my mind that my songs were good and that if I stayed with it long enough they would prove themselves."

Then came *Red Headed Stranger,* and everything changed for the performer. His rendition of "Blue Eyes Cryin' In The Rain" not only made the top country lists, it also merged with such disco/pop fare as "The Hustle" and "Love Will Keep Us Together" on the Top 40. The wide acceptance of "Blue Eyes" shoved the album all the way to gold status. It was merely a prelude to the next year's blockbuster called *The Outlaws*.

That collaborative effort by Willie, Waylon and his wife Jessi Colter, and Tompall Glaser slipped into the Top 10 on *Billboard*'s top pop albums. The album became the first country collection to reach officially certified platinum status.

After his pop breakthrough in 1976, Willie Nelson placed thirty-three albums on the top pop albums chart in the next ten years. In the five-year period from 1978 to 1983, of seventeen albums on the top pop chart, all but three early RCA albums went gold. Eight went platinum or multiplatinum. Five of Willie's albums stayed on the top pop albums chart more than a year, and *Stardust* remained on the chart more than two years. *Stardust* is one of two Willie Nelson albums with certified U.S. sales of more than three million copies. The other is *Always On My Mind,* which rated a top-five single on the Hot 100 and garnered a Grammy nomination for record of the year.

Willie Nelson's work has *lasting* appeal. That is why Willie is so successful in his theatrical movies. People are attracted to him as a person, and they can believe what he tells them.

An inebriated band member told biographer Bob Allen after a performance one night, while the tour bus trundled down the highway to the next night's show, that "Willie's the godfather. He's a good man. He's got an aura. He's got somethin' to say."

"Willie's like a lighthouse, like a preacher," says Gary Busey.

"Willie's like Buddha," says Kristofferson. "He's got a serenity about him that rubs off on you. I'm in awe of his peace."

To generations ten to twenty years younger than himself, Willie is a symbol of maturity. He shows no fear of growth or change, of new beginnings. He is still out there, on the road playing his music, making movies, and stirring up the nation's social conscience with Farm Aid I, II and III. Above all, he is still writing his incomparable songs.

"I think he will go down as one of the greatest, if not the greatest songwriter ever in country music . . . even greater than Hank Williams. He can write the most complex song, like 'And So Will You My Love,' that will shoot over most people's heads, and then he will turn around and write a little song like 'On the Road Again' that everybody can appreciate," says Waylon Jennings.

In 1986, Willie, Kristofferson, Waylon Jennings, and Johnny Cash — the Highwaymen — joined to remake John Ford's 1939 Western classic, *Stagecoach,* for television. It did nothing to diminish the stature of any of the stars, and Willie also served as executive producer of the film.

The dreams of the red-headed boy in the dusty, darkened theater in Abbott, of becoming a singing cowboy movie star, have acquired reality. But like others who became film stars after establishing themselves in other careers, Willie has mixed feelings about the movies. It means being tied to one location for long periods of time and a lot of plain sitting around, waiting for technicians to get the setup ready. To a man accustomed to 250–300 nights a year on the road, that can be debilitating confinement.

Of the future, Willie says, ''Mainly I'm goin' to play music, because that's what I really know how to do and what I enjoy doing more than anything else in the world. . . . Movies are fun, but . . . you can't get up and go somewhere every day. You have to get up and stay somewhere every day, and that goes against my grain a little.''

It is unlikely the singer's fans will allow him to stop making movies in the immediate future. As Waylon Jennings remarked, ''People down in Texas [and elsewhere] think when they die, they'll go to Willie's house.''

Willie Nelson has many close friends, but Kris Kristofferson is comfortably within the inner-inner circle. Born in Brownsville, three years later than Nelson, he grew up in that South Texas town before going to college in California. Then it was off to Oxford University where he earned a second degree in English and literature. Along the way he became a Golden Gloves boxer, wrote stories, and picked up a few habits that didn't serve him well as time went on. After serving a stint in the army as a helicopter pilot, Captain Kristofferson was discharged.

He flew helicopters delivering workers to oil rigs in the Gulf Coastal area, then headed for Nashville. From 1965 to 1969 he worked at oddjobs in Music City before dropping (literally) into Johnny Cash's back yard in a helicopter to pitch him a song. Cash recorded ''Sunday Morning Coming Down,'' and the rest, as they say, is history.

Kristofferson made his film debut in 1971 with a bit in *The Last Movie*. He starred the next year in *Cisco Pike*, followed the next year by several others. In 1974 he scored big in *Alice Doesn't Live Here Anymore*. He had made a dozen movies by 1986, including the one with Willie Nelson called *Songwriter*.

He has also done quite well in the TV movies he has made. But while he is a singer-songwriter from Texas like Nelson, he plays different kinds of roles, opposite stars as diverse as Barbra Streisand and Jane Fonda. And while Nelson is only three years older, he seems a father figure to Kristofferson.

Nevertheless, Kris has not been content to rely on his looks or fame as a songwriter to get by. With almost every movie, his skill in creating illusion has increased. And since he cleared his brain from the effects of drugs, his character range has broadened considerably.

Both Willie and Kris are deadly serious about their craft, whether as singers, songwriters, or actors. They bring an intensity to their work not found in many others, and refuse to accept less than their best efforts as creative artists. Further, they have the confidence, the tenacity, and the perseverance necessary for great accomplishment. Although both are in their fifties now, their best work as film stars lies ahead of them.

Another musician-actor with ability and serious intent is Gary Busey, from Goose Creek. He started his performing career as a drummer with The Rubber Band and stayed with that group about seven years. Then he joined Leon Russell's band under the name Teddy Jack Eddy. He also played drums for Kristofferson and Nelson.

Busey got his start in Hollywood when he was twenty-eight years old, in a film called *The Last American Hero*. Several other roles followed before he landed the lead in *The Buddy Holly Story* in 1978, a role which earned him an Academy Award nomination for Best Actor. In 1982 he made *Barbarosa* with Willie Nelson. He has since appeared in a television series, "The Texas Wheelers," and TV specials.

After winning *his* battle with drugs, Busey became even more active in moviemaking and has developed a substantial following among art-film folk. When that happens, it usually means an artist has decided to be serious. But Busey still has strong commercial appeal, and he actively appears in films that enhance his stature. As the body of his work increases, he is sure to achieve greater stardom.

A singer-songwriter from Lubbock, Mac Davis, has not yet appeared in a movie as a singer. He debuted in a Don Meredith-like role as a quarterback football player for the Dallas Bulls in *North Dallas Forty* (1979). Then other roles followed, including *Cheaper to Keep Her* (1980) and *Sting II* (1983). Davis has done a number of TV specials as a singer and host, but none strictly as an actor. He hasn't been as visible in recent years as in the early eighties. Mac

Davis has a winning and believable public persona. Finding the right roles for it takes a lot of time.

Although he was born in Florida, Pat Boone spent a substantial portion of his life in Texas, first in Fort Worth and then at college in Denton. There he was a classmate of singer Roy Orbison. Boone married the daughter of country singer Red Foley when he was nineteen and set about fathering four pretty daughters.

Pat Boone was a young man whose time had come. In 1957 he burst on the Hollywood scene with a 20th-Century contract and appeared in his first movie, *Bernardine*. He also appeared on TV that year as the star of "The Pat Boone Show." Movie followed movie, and in that innocent age, every one of them made money. *April Love, State Fair,* and *All Hands on Deck* give some idea of the subject matter. He was as wholesome and fresh as Elvis Presley was sexy and sensual, and each had his fans. Sometimes they shared them.

Unlike Presley, Pat Boone's image is squeaky clean, for the most part. Only rarely has any gossip touched his name. But a few years ago, he admitted to straying some from the home pasture. Apparently all was forgiven and he mended his ways — maybe not in that order.

Yet another Texas native has made musical legend and trekked to Hollywood: Kenny Rogers.

Born into a poor family that included eight children, Kenny had his first band before he was eighteen. It was called, appropriately enough, The Scholars, and he netted $13 from their first professional engagement.

Musically precocious, his record of "That Crazy Feeling" went gold, and he appeared on Dick Clark's "American Bandstand" when he was twenty. The following year, he joined a Houston jazz group called The Bobby Doyle Trio and played a stand-up bass with that ensemble. Wanting to get out of Houston and to be with a national group, he joined The New Christy Minstrels in 1965 and toured the country. When that group dissolved in 1967, he and three other Christy Minstrel members formed a band called The First Edition. They signed with Frank Sinatra's Reprise label, and appeared on "The Smothers Brothers Comedy Hour" and "The Ed Sullivan Show."

The First Edition enjoyed great success for the next five years, producing hits such as "Just Dropped In (To See What Condition My Condition Was In)" and "But You Know I Love You." "Ruby, Don't Take Your Love To Town" hit just the right note for the times, and Kenny Rogers and The First Edition were favorites of Vietnam-era youngsters. The group hosted its own syndicated TV variety show, "Rollin'," in 1972, and went on a world tour. They stayed together until 1975, when Kenny Rogers developed his solo act and signed with United Artists Records.

"Lucille," a single from his 1976 solo album, *Kenny Rogers*, went gold and won Rogers a Grammy for Best Country Vocal Performance. Both *Kenny Rogers* and his next album, *Daytime Friends*, earned gold designations. In 1978 he won four Academy of Country Music awards. Rogers then released three new albums, including *The Gambler*, which also led to his first television movie.

Awards piled on awards. Success followed success. Unfortunately, divorce also followed divorce.

He did his first television spectacular, "A Special Kenny Rogers" for CBS in 1979. After the Academy of Country Music named him Entertainer of the Year, he made a second TV special, "Kenny Rogers and the American Cowboy," again for CBS.

Kenny Rogers's first venture into movie acting was more than successful. His acting debut in "Kenny Rogers as The Gambler" won the highest ratings on any TV movie that year. In the fall, his new album, *Greatest Hits*, contained Lionel Ritchie's "Lady." It topped the pop charts for six weeks and shot the album's sales to more than 12 million, worldwide. Another TV special, "Kenny Rogers' America," was shown on CBS the fall of 1980. The next year, Rogers played a preacher in "Coward of the County," and that TV movie also received the highest ratings of the year.

Nineteen eighty-two was not without a little rain, however. Rogers made his first theatrical film, *Six Pack*, that year, and it was a failure. For some reason, audiences didn't find him believable as a race car driver. Also, there is a great difference between TV movie audiences and theatrical film audiences, and producers/directors/stars who don't take those differences into account frequently — usually — get rudely jostled. Kenny has not made a theatrical film since.

Rogers signed with RCA in 1983, and his first album release, *Eyes That See In the Dark*, included the biggest single in the history of

RCA Records: his duet with Dolly Parton, "Islands in the Stream," which sold over 2 million single copies.

Also in 1983 he filmed a two-part miniseries called "Kenny Rogers as The Gambler: The Adventure Continues." The series earned large ratings. Just as he was believed when he sang the song that spawned the films, so was he accepted in the title role of the films. In mid-November, *Wild Horses*, another Kenny Rogers TV movie, aired on CBS television. It co-starred David Andrews, Pam Dawber, Richard Farnsworth, and Ben Johnson. He wrote a couple of songs especially for the film, "Eight Second Hero" and the theme music called "Wild Horses." The movie drew respectable audiences, but not the huge one he might have expected, given the great success of the "Gambler" series.

"My best chance in movies is to be like John Wayne," he told an interviewer in Sheridan, Wyoming, where *Horses* was filmed. "I don't really consider myself an actor, just like I don't really consider myself a singer. I can sing, but there are other singers, and I can act, but there are other actors. If you give me believable dialogue in a believable situation, I can keep it believable. And I suppose not a lot of people can do that."

His complaints about moviemaking are much the same as other singers-musicians. "I enjoy acting," he says, "but I hate the hanging around. The days on movie sets are long, and it's very disruptive to my family."

Yet Kenny Rogers seems driven to be successful in movies — TV or otherwise. "What happens in this business," observed Rogers, "is that you're given a certain number of years when you can generate a certain amount of income. And I feel I need to get it while it's there. I genuinely enjoy doing what I do, and even if I had twice as much money as I have, I would still enjoy working."

The Houston native's acting range is admittedly limited. "I don't want to play psychopaths or drug dealers. I have no desire to be a comedian. If I could do a film like *Rocky* that generates hundreds of millions, then perhaps it would allow me to be more versatile."

For such an exceedingly wealthy man, Kenny Rogers seems to inspire no jealousy. Although he sinks big bucks into cars and homes, when he sells them, he does so at a profit.

But Rogers and his wife, Marianne, put money back into the community too. They have been involved in World Hunger projects for over half a decade, as well as other charitable purposes. He was particularly instrumental in the "We Are the World" project to raise money for starving Africans.

Country singers, or any kind of entertainers, for that matter, tend to have serial marriages. Kenny Rogers is no exception. In a television interview in late 1986, he addressed the problems associated with his previous marriages, and the joy he has found in the present one. They are the sort of problems any man of nearly fifty years might experience at some time in his life: emotional immaturity, insecurity, not knowing who one is. But mostly he blames his failed marriages on his single-minded devotion to professional success. He said his song "Music Man" is his own voice addressing himself, and it sums up his disastrous early experiences. Basically, the song is about a person not being true to himself, to his own inner core.

Once he took off his bronze-lensed glasses, removed the ring from his ear, changed his clothing to some more appropriate for a man his age, and quit trying to be twenty-five years old forever, Rogers says, his life changed. He was happier. He was being himself, and the world approved. Fame and fortune sought him out. He awoke one morning to find a beautiful wife beside him that he could love and be faithful to, and a young son he could hold and cherish. He is now on the road only twenty-five nights a year.

Kenny Rogers knows what it is like to be Texas-poor, to grow up in a $35-a-month Houston Heights project with an alcoholic father. He doesn't ever want to be that way again. But, if asked, he would trade it all for the peace and serenity he has found with his current family, and he never misses an opportunity to tell the world.

How does he account for his success? "I'm not a great singer or a vocal technician . . . my talent is sort of unobvious. I'm a stylist. An entertainer. I have a familiar voice with a certain honesty, and distinction," he told an interviewer.

Those words could apply equally well to Willie Nelson. Or Bing Crosby. Or Gene Autry. All men who became fabulously wealthy as an outgrowth of their singing-songwriting-acting careers.

The Era of
Small-Screen Stardom

Fabulous Fifties is a term that doesn't apply to the movie industry. Credit court-ordered divestiture of the studios' theater chains, Joe McCarthy's Communist witchhunt, and television with the demise of the movie business as it had been known. A smaller number of Texans became established in Hollywood during the decade than in any since the advent of filmmaking.

But those few who found the industry slackening didn't give up. With Texan determination, they turned toward the stage, singing careers, or that new little box called television to prove their talents.

Dorothy Malone, a good-looking Dallasite, won a Best Supporting Actress Oscar for her role as a frustrated nymphomaniac in *Written on the Wind* (1956). But her most popular role was probably as a star in the TV series "Peyton Place." Malone has had many other interests and careers besides acting, and she intersperses movie roles with others when she returns to Dallas.

Arriving in Hollywood at about the same time as Dorothy Malone was the dancer considered by cognoscenti to have the best legs ever seen in a community not known for coarse ones.

A dancer-friend of Mary Martin's by the name of Nico Charisse used to swing through Weatherford to visit Martin on trips from New York to California. Through a fortuitous set of circumstances that occurred on one of these diversions to Texas, Charisse became the ballet instructor of Tula Ellice Finklea from Amarillo. He soon married her, and having gone with him to Hollywood, she became a bit player under the name Lily Norwood. But success eluded her until she got a contract at MGM, where she became the beautiful, leggy, popular screen star and dance partner of Fred Astaire and Gene Kelly.

Cyd Charisse, as she became known, joined Ann Miller and Debbie Reynolds as the three Texan survivors when the movie business went bust in the late fifties and sixties. Charisse performs on television and in live cabaret now with her husband of several decades, Tony Martin.

The Unsinkable Debbie Reynolds, an El Paso native, earned forty-eight merit badges as a Girl Scout. When her marriage to Eddie Fisher went kaput, the movies went broke, and MGM went down the drain, Debbie Reynolds put her scout training to use and was well prepared and resourceful. She went on the road with a club act and now performs regularly on television, claiming that each year is going to be the final one. It hasn't happened yet.

The Blonde Bombshell named Jayne Mansfield (whom no one would *ever* call *plain*) would do anything to become a movie star. And did. By the fifties, the definitions of fame, glamour, and stardom had changed considerably since the early days of filmmaking. But whatever it took, Jayne Mansfield wanted it all. She ultimately became a caricature of herself before it ended with her decapitation in an automobile accident.

But Jayne, not plain, and not dumb either (with an IQ in the low genius range), reflected the confusion rampant in the film industry in the late days of the decade. It would be a while before order was restored.

The sixties were even sorrier for filmmakers than the fifties. The industry was in almost total disarray and produced only a few bright new faces from Texas. Carol Burnett, an endearing and enduring star of comedy and lately drama, grew in popularity during this time. Her variety show on television was one of the most watched programs of its kind to date. Through her show, Burnett's reputation grew into a film career. Her successful roles have continued her comedic reputation and have solidly planted her as a serious dramatic actress.

Burnett, as well as many other Texans, took advantage of the Age of Television — an era that really has not ended yet.

Not all Texans who went west to Eden did so to pursue a career in theatrical films. Since the mid-fifties, many have specifically selected the small screen. In some cases, actors realistically could not expect to land a job in the movies, but believed they could get into television. This condition was especially true in the early days of the medium. (A career in television today is professionally acceptable. But in the beginning, TV occupied the same second-best position relative to films that beginning filmmakers initially occupied relative to the stage.) As theatrical film production in the late fifties and early sixties diminished nearly to the point of no return, there were no other options than to go into television.

The first Texan star to make it big in television was tiny Josephine Owaissa Cottle. She was born in Bloomington, Texas, during a spring storm in 1921. When she became an actress, she called herself Gale Storm.

Gale won Jesse Lasky's "Gateway to Hollywood" talent search in 1939, but she was dropped by RKO after a heartbreakingly short six months. From there she went to small-change Monogram Studio, where she made several Westerns with Roy Rogers, then to Universal, where she appeared with Audie Murphy and Dan Duryea, among others. As far as the film industry was concerned, however, Gale Storm was a member of the faceless crowd of would-be stars.

But then along came television. Her first series, "My Little Margie," was one of the most popular situation comedies on TV from 1952 to 1955, and it is still seen in syndication around the world.

Next came "Oh, Susanna," changed to "The Gale Storm Show" after its first popular season. The show dealt with the misadventures of the social director of the luxury liner SS *Ocean Queen*. Gale, naturally, was the social director. The show appeared three seasons on CBS, and then moved to ABC to run for another three years, finally ending in 1962. Since those two popular shows, Gale Storm has rarely worked in television.

The Texan actress did not have to rely solely on acting in her earlier career. She could sing. Her 1955 recording of "I Hear You Knocking" was for some time the second most popular record in the country. Her "Teen-Age Prayer" was on the hit charts for fifteen weeks straight that same year. In 1957, "Dark Moon" made *Billboard*'s Top 100 list for twenty-three weeks.

Her fame is still widespread today because of reruns of her old TV shows. When she chooses to work dinner theaters in plays such as *The Unsinkable Molly Brown* or *Cactus Flower,* her appearances command substantial fees. She has no financial need to work, but does not consider herself retired.

Gale Storm's major Texas contribution to television, besides a lot of innocent fun, has been as one of the earliest comediennes to grasp what the new TV audiences wanted in entertainment provided by women. That is no small attainment, when you consider how few women comics there were in the early days of television.

Carolyn Jones received an Academy Award nomination for *The Bachelor Party* in 1957, when she was only twenty-four. She went on to become a versatile film actress, successfully playing a wide variety of offbeat roles. But in spite of her numerous film accomplishments, and they are substantial, Jones may be best known for her portrayal of the morbidly beautiful Morticia in TV's "The Addams Family." The show was based on the Charles Addams cartoons published in *The New Yorker* magazine for many years. Morticia and husband Gomez preside over a macabre family whose ghoulish ways parody the normal world. Morticia cultivates roses for the thorns instead of the blooms.

Critics jumped on the series when it premiered in September 1964, claiming the show missed the real point of Addams's cartoons. But the public loved the show. They particularly enjoyed Morticia's outlandish makeup and weird clothing. Carolyn even died her naturally blonde hair to black for the role. She played in other fine television presentations, including one of husband Aaron Spelling's plays, *The Last Man* on "Playhouse 90," and in one of his episodes for the "Zane Grey Theater." Nevertheless, Carolyn Jones was Morticia for most fans.

She had married Aaron Spelling in 1953, and the marriage lasted eleven years. The parting was amicable, and the couple worked together many times after their divorce.

The daughter of a branch manager for Allis-Chalmers farm machinery in Amarillo, Carolyn Jones died of cancer in California in

1983. She said of her life in Eden: "I like Hollywood and I like being a movie star. Hollywood has been very good to me."

One slow-talking man made a great success wearing a coonskin hat and a leather outfit. Fess Parker of Fort Worth — the rugged, wholesome leading man of action films — also became the TV and big-screen incarnation of Davy Crockett, Daniel Boone, and other pioneer heroes. Parker is retired from show business now and is living in Santa Barbara, where he conducts extensive real estate operations.

The "Sausage King" of Texas, and possibly the rest of the country, too, was born on a farm near Seth Ward, Texas — a little piece down the road from Plainview. In 1928, no less than today, it was the heart of cotton, grain, and alfalfa country. And for the Dean family, it was pitifully poor country.

Jimmy "Big Bad John" Dean had a daddy who ran away not long after Jimmy's younger brother was born, and a mother who took up barbering to support the family. Jimmy never knew much of his father, but he knew a lot about his other parent. "They don't make 'em outta that kinda stock anymore," he avers in a voice with a hard edge. Her example, as well as his grandfather's, made him determined to make something of himself and forged in him a strong and honest individualism. It also made him determined to participate in the American dream.

"Kids used to laugh at my clothes, my bib overalls and galluses because we were dirt poor. And I'd go home and tell Mom how miserable I felt being laughed at. I dreamt of havin' a beautiful home, a nice car, nice clothes. . . . I wanted to be *somebody*," he said.

Dean became a singer quite easily and naturally, almost as soon as he learned to speak. Musical instruments came easily to him too. His mother had taken a piano course by correspondence, so she was able to teach him. Later he taught himself to play the harmonica, the guitar, and the accordion.

His first professional job was playing the accordion in a tavern near the air force base where he was stationed. At $4 a night, he decided show business might not be a bad way to make a living. He formed an instrumental quartet with three other airmen, and they would play rowdy honky-tonks in the Washington, D.C. area for $8 a night, plus tips. After he was discharged in 1948, Dean stayed in the area and continued to perform as singer, accordionist, and hayseed comedian. One night the most successful country-music impresario on the East Coast caught his act and signed him to a contract.

Starting on radio, Dean and his group, The Texas Wildcats, soon moved into regional television. Their popularity enabled them to play country and state fairs, and his recordings began to move. "Bummin' Around" in 1953 brought him a national reputation. The group quickly moved up to larger programs and bigger production features. Tapes of Dean's radio shows were broadcast by more than a thousand stations across the country, and films of his TV shows were syndicated nationally to about forty stations.

Early in 1957, CBS hired Dean and the boys to compete against the "Today Show" on NBC for the first forty-five minutes — from 7:00 to 7:45. The "Jimmy Dean Show," his first network television outing, received 25,000 fan letters a week. CBS's ratings went higher than they had ever been, but no sponsor could be found and the network dropped the show. However, they bought Dean's contract from the impresario and planned to use him in something else.

The network took him to New York for an afternoon show but tried to take the country out of the boy, which one cannot do. They tried to force on him a pop format alien to his style. The day before the show's premiere, Jimmy walked out of rehearsals and "bawled [his] head off" for about thirty minutes. "They're barking up the wrong tree if they want a sophisticated boy in a sophisticated atmosphere. I'll always be a country boy, no matter what happens," he said of that trial. He remembered what his mama had told him a thousand times as he was growing up in Seth Ward: "Be yourself, 'cause if people don't like you as yourself, they're sure not going to like you as somebody you're trying to be."

The network compromised some, but not enough, and dropped the show at the end of the season. It was three years before Dean returned to television. During the interval, he played to capacity crowds at fairs and in coliseums. He also gave more attention to his recordings. During this time he wrote "Big Bad John," which sold more than a million copies during the next months. It had the biggest sale of any single in the recording industry for several years.

When Jack Paar left the "Tonight Show" in early 1962, the network used interim hosts for twenty-nine weeks until the permanent appointment of Johnny Carson. One week in July, Jimmy Dean was the interim host. His honest, folksy, easygoing manner suited the audience to a tee. Only one other host received a higher rating during the interim period.

NBC wanted to keep Dean but had nothing at the moment. Luckily, ABC did, and the "Jimmy Dean Show" opened December 21, 1962. At first, ABC tried to do the same thing CBS had done. Ratings were low, and before long, the closing notice went up. Jimmy begged network executives to let him be himself, to fail or succeed on his own merits, not somebody else's. Feeling there was little to lose, the network finally let him try it. After several weeks, the ratings started up and the closing notice came down. The show was on its way. It ran for three seasons before syndication, and that at Dean's request. He wanted to do other things.

Although Jimmy Dean likes show business, he told a *New York Post* reporter in September 1963: "I'm not a dyed-in-the-wool show person. I don't *run* with show people."

Dean did keep active in entertainment, however, as he developed business interests. He has had investments in real estate, golf ranges, publishing, and many other areas. But he is perhaps most widely known in business circles for his Jimmy Dean Sausage, with corporate headquarters located nowhere else but in Dallas, Texas.

Country music variety shows prospered after Dean's show, and most of the favorites featured Texans. The list includes Roger Miller, Buck Owens, the Mandrell Sisters, and Kenny Rogers.

Sunny Sandy Duncan — veteran of countless commercials, game shows, specials, talk shows, the star of her own series, winner of an Emmy for her dramatic role in the series "Roots" — is clearly a television personality. There is little she hasn't accomplished in the medium.

As a result, Sandy Duncan has recently confined herself, for the most part, to the stage. Although she has appeared in a couple of well received Disney movies, that medium doesn't seem to be of much interest to her.

Sandra Duncan is a product of East Texas — born in Henderson because that is where the hospital was, but the family lived in a small community called Overton. By the time she was ready for school, her family had moved to Tyler, which lies due west from Henderson.

When she was about four, she climbed up on the American Legion stage where a dance recital was in progress and would not come down until her mother promised she could have dance lessons herself. "This thing about performing was always in me," says Sandy.

The remainder of her childhood was filled with performing. But she didn't let her dancing, singing, and drama lessons interfere with academics. She compiled a straight-A record at Robert E. Lee High School in Tyler. After a couple of years at Lon Morris Junior College, where she concentrated on drama, she was ready for New York. By then she had performed in leading roles every year at the Texas State Fair Music Hall.

She bunked in Manhattan's Rehearsal Club, a residence for single aspiring actresses, along with Diane Keaton and Blythe Danner. As the small parts grew, along with favorable notices, she won parts in road shows, started doing television commercials, and got her career established. She also went on a couple of tours to Vietnam.

In 1970, appearing in a revival of *The Boy Friend,* she won her second Tony nomination, a New York Drama Desk Award, and an Outer Critics Circle Award for the 1969–70 season's best performance in a musical. Katharine Hepburn and Lauren Bacall were also in musicals that season.

Having seen *The Boy Friend,* shrewd Fred Silverman offered Duncan her own television series. He was at that time programing executive for CBS-TV. In an interview, he compared Sandy's poise to that of Audrey Hepburn; her calculated mannerisms to those of Katharine Hepburn or Bette Davis; her superb comedic timing to that of Carol Burnett; and her antic energy to that of Debbie Reynolds. The series, called "Funny Face," borrowed its title alone from the Fred Astaire-Audrey Hepburn movie.

In the series, Sandy played a pert UCLA student working her way through college to become an actress. Although critics grumbled at the weakness of the premise, audiences loved the show immediately. It made Sandy Duncan a nationally recognized star overnight and earned her an Emmy nomination. The show ranked eighth in the Nielsen ratings. It looked as if Sandy had arrived in Eden.

Instead, it was pure hell. During filming of the first thirteen episodes, the Texan had suffered painful headaches, and physicians decided to do a complete examination to determine the cause. They found a walnut-sized fibroid tumor behind her left eye, pressing against the optic nerve. The doctors had to remove a portion of her skull to carefully cut away the growth. It took them seven and a half hours. In order to do the job, her left optic nerve was cut, and she permanently lost vision in that eye. That was the end of "Funny Face."

Network execs got together a new show for the Texas trouper to debut the following season (1972) called "The Sandy Duncan Show." It didn't click in the ratings, and the show was canceled after three months. Duncan was sorry, of course, but for other than the obvious reasons.

"So much of what you do on television is in the hands of others. It doesn't rise or fall on your merits at all — that scares me most," she said.

But she wasn't finished with television. For the next six years, she made just about every talk show, commercial, game show, appearance in others' series, and numerous one-shot specials of her own that she could cram in. The reason for the talk and game shows, she says, was to give publicity to whatever it was she was *really* doing at the time.

Of the three media in which she has worked, Duncan says: "TV is hardest, a grind. Theater is a daily ego trip with all that applause. Movies are the most creative, because a mood is concocted out of time sequence, and all those closeups really zoom in on acting expressions."

But the theater is her first love. She even had the courage to attempt the unthinkable: Mary Martin's *Peter Pan*. She didn't try to ape Martin's Peter, however, favoring her own interpretation. She brought out the darker side of childhood, the "broody, scary side to Peter." According to Duncan, "There's a lot of violence in him, and he lies and makes up things. And . . . he's a survivor — like me." She said the Martin version of the fifties was the result of a sweeter, more innocent time.

The play opened on Broadway in 1979 to generally enthusiastic reviews. *Variety*'s critic said: "It would be hard to imagine better casting than Sandy Duncan as Peter Pan. Her boyish, pixie quality is a natural." Jack Kroll of *Newsweek* said it should run as long as there are kids in New York.

Sandy continues to work on Broadway, quite frequently with Tommy Tune, a native of Wichita Falls. They talk about Wichita Falls weather when things get tough on stage.

Her first marriage to a fellow actor ended in 1971 after three years, then she married a physician who was on staff at UCLA Medical Center where she underwent surgery. Her third husband is dancer Don Correia, whom she married on July 21, 1980.

As far as her current career goes, the offers continue to come her way. Considering all she has achieved, it's easy to see why.

With so many fine performers from Texas working in television, selection is inevitably the major problem in writing about them. One thinks of fine singers such as Barbara and Louise Mandrell. Or Mac Davis. Or Roger Miller, who, in addition to having his own show, has written many fine songs and won numerous awards, including Tonys for Broadway production writing. Or Buck Owens, who has had the longest-running weekly format around in "Hee Haw."

Or more recent actors such as Lee Horsley from Muleshoe, who did a fine job on "Matt Houston." Randy Quaid gave a masterful portrayal of LBJ in a miniseries in 1987. John Hillerman toils splendidly as Tom Selleck's sidekick in "Magnum, P.I." And young Lisa Whelchel is already a veteran in "Facts of Life." The Angel Jaclyn Smith works steadily in movie after movie for television. Phylicia Rashad is extremely popular in "The Cosby Show," and her sister, dancing Debbie Allen, has parlayed her talents into movies and the TV series "Fame." Morgan Fairchild's beginnings in television led to several film roles.

Perhaps the most memorable character in television of recent times — and maybe of all times — is a Texan who plays a Texan.

In May of 1980, more than a quarter of a billion people throughout the world began to wait out the long summer hiatus to discover "Who Shot J.R.?" As it turned out, an actors' strike prolonged the agony of uncertainty until late in the new season. When the truth was known, audiences learned that the attempted murder was committed by the character played by a Texan-once-removed, Mary Catharine Crosby, daughter of

Houston's Kathy Grant and Bing Crosby. Only one other American TV show outpointed "Dallas" that year — the Super Bowl. But worldwide, "Dallas" won hands down.

In only two seasons, the series became the most watched television show in the world. The star: Weatherford's Larry Hagman. The setting: Dallas, of course. The theme: Texas mystique. And no one better epitomized that mystique than J. R. Ewing, as played by Hagman.

While traits such as courage, honesty, openness, and independence had been admired in the nineteenth-century Texas cowboy, his virtual antithesis, the oil baron, became the twentieth-century incarnation of the Texan myth. He was someone who strikes it rich overnight, someone who's mighty lucky. He may also be ruthless, cruel, unscrupulous, devious, and unfaithful. In "Dallas," elements of the cowboy myth and oil baron myth are combined.

Place an authentic Texan in the lead role who comprehends the myths and exemplifies them, and you have a megahit. And not just among Texans, who enjoy watching their bigger-than-life portrayal as much as anybody else, but throughout this country and the rest of the industrial world. Even in Third World countries, the success of "Dallas" and its star is incredible. In the spring of 1987, 390 million viewers worldwide watched the show each week. Nothing in television's past presaged it, and nothing has superseded it.

Larry Hagman did not draw on personal success to develop J. R. Ewing's persona. In fact, his career had fallen into a deep trough when Lorimar offered him the then secondary role of Bobby Ewing's older brother. He refused the role three times. After all, the money was not that good, and he was a star. Lorimar made one final offer, and on the advice of Hagman's wife of twenty-odd years, he accepted. Maj Hagman knew how miserable her husband was, not working regularly, and she saw potential in the character. Besides, they needed the money.

Hagman was born into a prominent Weatherford family whose ancestors included judges, lawyers, and an assistant Texas attorney general. His mother, Mary Martin, was wed scarcely a month when she became pregnant. When Larry was born, she was still two months shy of her eighteenth birthday. And she wanted to be an actress and dancer more than anything in the world — including being a mother. As a consequence, Larry spent a lot of time in private and military schools as a child, frequently far from his mother and father, who divorced after a few years. Ben Hagman's horizons reached as far east as Fort Worth and Dallas, and perhaps Mineral Wells to the west, but not much farther. He was quite successful as a small-town attorney in Weatherford, and that is exactly what and where he wanted to be.

Larry didn't hit it off with his mother's second husband, Richard Halliday, a story editor in Hollywood. Halliday devoted himself to managing Martin's career after their marriage, and he and his stepson never developed a close relationship throughout the long marriage. Hagman lived with his maternal grandmother in Los Angeles until she died in 1944. He then stayed with the Hallidays awhile, and eventually lived with Halliday's mother in Connecticut. In 1946, Mary Martin contracted to appear in a London production and wanted her son to come along. He was willing enough, until he discovered that the fashionable Savoy Hotel, where they would be staying, wouldn't let him wear his cowboy boots in the lobby. No dice, he decided.

Besides, he missed the rest of his family. As a teenager he went back to Weatherford to live with his father, stepmother, and younger brother Gary. It was altogether an amicable relationship, and Larry's years at Weatherford High School were not greatly different from those of any other student from a relatively well-to-do family. His dad did buy him a surplus jeep, however, while most other boys his age were pleased to ride motor scooters. The jeep gave him a certain status the others didn't enjoy, and more mobility, a desirable condition in the wide open spaces of West Texas.

In that part of Texas, at least back in the forties, sons of he-men played football or boxed in the Golden Gloves. Sometimes both. Larry chose gloves. His coach and trainer was an ambitious young state legislator named Jim Wright, destined to rise to political heights.

When mother Mary offered to take Larry to England, it was with the understanding he could work in some capacity in her production and learn the trade. Larry hadn't wanted a theatrical career then. He wanted to wear cowboy boots, and in high school he gave serious thought to becoming a veterinarian or a circus performer who worked with animals. But a couple of summers spent under the North Central Texas sun, baling hay and digging septic tanks, convinced him he had a calling to show business. He took the money he had saved and rode the Greyhound to New York, determined to pursue a stage career.

Larry reestablished his relationship with his mother, and it blossomed. She was delighted that he had decided to go on the stage, and she helped him get started, to the extent that he allowed it.

Later, a tour in the Air Force resulted in meeting his one and only wife, Maj Axelsson, whom he married in England on his twenty-third birthday. She thought he acted rather "odd" at that time, but said he "matured a lot" later. When his enlistment ended, Larry and Maj went to Hollywood, where Hagman established himself as a man of honor and integrity. He also soon proved he was possessed by the self-perfection habit, like his mother, a trait that caused him trouble along the way when he extended the application of it to others.

For several years in the fifties, Hagman worked in the daytime soap opera "Edge of Night" and also appeared in several films. But it was the mid-sixties before he became a recognized star as Major Tony Nelson in "I Dream of Jeannie," co-starring Barbara Eden. The series lasted five seasons and is still in syndication.

Larry hadn't saved much money, and he had alienated many of his co-workers with his perfectionist attitude. Most important for the future, his contract didn't give him royalties when the series was syndicated. He was in a tight corner when the show ended, and it got tighter.

It took seven years before he overcame the way casting directors perceived him. During those lean years, Hagman's earnings reached an all-time low, and he spent $40,000 undergoing analysis. To keep the family's head above water, Maj designed clothing and hot tub spas. When Larry got an occasional job, Maj would travel to the studio from their little house in Santa Monica, bringing her husband's lunch in a brown bag.

Such was the state of their affairs when Lorimar offered the role of J. R. to Hagman in the fall of 1977. Personally, he possessed none of the attributes of J. R. Ewing, other than the fact that they were both Texans.

No one has accused Larry Hagman of being a bad guy, but playing a rich, powerful character, unfettered by ordinary constraints, *has* given him an expanded sense of possibilities. "Dallas" entered the sweepstakes in 1978 in fifty-eighth place. By the end of the season, it had reached seventh place. And at the end of the 1979–80 season, the show was number one. Hagman had clearly established himself as the star, and rivaled Alan Alda as the most popular male star in television.

When a quarter of a billion people care whether a character you created lives or dies, Larry felt, it is time to renegotiate your contract. Hagman spent the summer of 1980 touring England and Europe as the "one-and-only, irreplaceable J.R." He had three agents haggling with Lorimar at the time; he made all three wear white hats. Lorimar countered the white hats by threatening to have Robert Culp ready to emerge from a burning ambulance, undergo plastic surgery, and re-emerge as J. R. Ewing. But Lorimar didn't have to carry out the threat. Hagman's salary was raised to $75,000 per episode, three times as much as he got the preceding year and considerably more than the sum he received at the beginning of his contract.

Season after season, "Dallas" rolled up huge ratings and even bigger revenues. Hagman became indispensable. Jim Davis as Papa Jock could die, but the series would continue. Charlene Tilton or Patrick Duffy could leave, and the show would go on. If Victoria Principal doesn't get as much money as the men on the show, she will go. But the show won't stop.

"I keep telling 'em, we've got five, six years left, if we play it right," says Hagman. But that eventuality holds only if Hagman continues to be J. R. Ewing.

In 1984 Hagman began renegotiating his contract without excessive demands or threats. He did say, however, that if he did not get what he wanted, he would resort to having his recreational vehicle parked on the lot, a contractual right. That meant Lorimar would have to provide a teamster driver twelve hours a day, which equals $2,000 a week. Multiply that by thirteen, if the other stars demanded it, and that would work out to nearly $30,000 a week in extra production expenses.

"I haven't had to play that card yet, but the threat is always there," says Hagman, smiling his J. R. smile.

He now earns about $3 million a year for "Dallas" alone, not counting syndication royalties. But he always remembers that in 1976, the year before signing to do "Dallas," he was forced to rent out his Malibu home for the summer to generate cash flow. And he had to move his family to his mother's home in

Palm Springs, where he slept until 5:00 P.M. each day to escape the 110-degree heat.

"It was a disorienting time," he said later. During that time he learned two things: he didn't want to be poor, and he wanted to live in his own home in Malibu.

In early spring of 1986, when things were not going particularly well for the series, Hagman blamed it all on the executive producer of the show. Philip Capice held firmly to an international storyline which was not attracting new viewers and was causing some old-faithfuls to jump ship. And Capice had forced Leonard Katzman — "the real brains behind the show" — to leave his job as producer. Under Capice, "We have all this foreign glitter, when what people want from 'Dallas' is a focus on the family," said Hagman. He wanted Philip Capice fired.

Lorimar–Telepictures Entertainment president Lee Rich said no thanks. Hagman began openly deriding Capice in front of the crew and came to the defense of his friends who had conflicts with Capice. After playing J. R. Ewing for eight years, he had become, to some extent, the character he portrayed. The years of adulation, recognition, and high-rolling had brought about more of the real-life trappings of the Texas oil baron, and he didn't mind flexing his muscle. He wanted Katzman back in creative control to assure the future of the show.

Lee Rich issued a sharp warning when he heard Hagman's goal. "No performer is going to run this show," he said. "I just wish [Larry Hagman] would give me an ultimatum. That would be the end of the show. This is none of Larry's damn business."

Several weeks later, Lorimar-Telepictures announced that Capice would be gone at the end of the season, and that Leonard Katzman would become the new executive producer.

"They want you to be the character, and you feel that, and sometimes you slip into it," said Hagman, explaining how fans perceive him in public. "They see you as him, and after a while you find the character is you. You think, I guess I am J. R. as much as J. R. is me."

At the end of the 1986–87 season, "Dallas" was firmly back in the top ten circle of shows. J. R. Ewing was tall in the saddle, as only he can be.

It's awfully hard for folks to get too much of the Texas mystique.

While television stars gained recognition and popularity in the small-screen era, the period offered time for several serious Texan actors and directors to put high gloss on their techniques. What they have proven is that Lone Star natives mean business these days.

Striving for What Matters

Bad luck may be responsible for one of the most illustrious careers of any actress in Hollywood. When she was sixteen, with her brother dying of leukemia, her parents sent Sissy Spacek to New York to spend the summer with cousin Rip Torn and his actress wife, Geraldine Page. The idea was to spare Sissy the ordeal of watching her brother's decline and ultimate death. But the visit also set on fire the desire in Spacek's soul to be an entertainer, specifically, a rock singer. She had already learned to play the guitar back home on her $14.95 Sears Roebuck special.

After finishing her last year at Quitman High School, where she had been a cheerleader, majorette, and homecoming queen, Sissy spent two days on the University of Texas campus before convincing her parents to let her skip college and return to New York. She spent several years trying to crack the rock scene, supporting herself by making commercials, singing backup on jingles, and working in a boutique gift shop. Finally, a young agent persuaded her to concentrate on acting, and before long she picked up an extra part in Andy Warhol's *Trash*, then a bit in *Prime Cut*. It was two years after that before she got her first real break in a low-budget art film called *Badlands*, written, produced, and directed by Texan Terrence Malick. She played the female lead opposite Martin

Sheen in the story of mankiller Charles Starkweather and his girl-friend, Caril Ann Fugate. Critics called her portrayal "resplendently promising."

Two years of relative obscurity descended upon the actress, broken only by a few appearances in TV movies. Then Brian de Palma starred her in a gothic film called *Carrie* that drew raves from the critics. The National Society of Film Critics named her the best actress of 1976, surpassing even Liv Ullman and Faye Dunaway. She also was nominated for an Academy Award for the same film, but Dunaway won.

A pair of attention-getting films followed in 1977. One was Robert Altman's *Three Women*, starring Texan Shelley Duvall, for which Sissy won the New York Film Critics' best supporting actress award. Altman said of her performance: "She is as good an actress as I've ever seen work," one who "is able to become whatever you ask her to transmit." The other film, by Altman protégé Alan Rudolph, was *Welcome to LA*. The critics panned it, but not the acting by Spacek.

More television work followed. And then, in 1980, her portrayal of country singer Loretta Lynn in *The Coal Miner's Daughter*, opposite Texan Tommy Lee Jones, was good enough to capture the Academy Award for Best Actress. Since then, she has been nominated for three more film roles: in *Missing* (1982), where she co-starred with Oscar-winner Jack Lemmon; in *The River* (1984), as Mae Garvey opposite Mel Gibson; and in 1986 as Babe MaGrath Botrelle in *Crimes of the Heart*, where her co-stars were Oscar-winners Diane Keaton and Jessica Lange.

The blistering pace set by Spacek in winning Academy Award nominations is the hottest in the history of the Oscars. The all-time winner, Katharine Hepburn, didn't receive her fifth nomination until she was forty-four years of age, compared with Spacek's thirty-six. Also, Spacek has appeared in only fourteen theatrical films. It took many more for Hepburn to get five nominations. But the sheer numerical comparison is not the most significant factor.

During the thirties and forties, there was in moviemaking a subgenre known as "women's films." Many women screenwriters turned out the scripts for those films, and certain directors were known as "women's directors." One of the best and most famous of these directors was Academy Award-winner George Cukor. But since the early sixties, the demand for women's films has diminished. Part of the reason is the breakup of the old studio system which created glamorous stars. Also to blame is the rise of working women, which eliminated the draw of women to afternoon matinees to see their favorite female stars. Now afternoon soaps and evening sitcoms have taken over the demand for intimate female-oriented drama.

The present image of women in American society is unclear. Old stereotypes don't hold anymore, but the new woman's role is not certain, either. If Hollywood loves anything, it is certainty, and so producers are reluctant to take chances until the image of the modern woman becomes more coherent. Until that happens, there will be few great women's pictures.

Katharine Hepburn received her first five nominations (one award) over a period of eighteen years during the heyday of women's films. Sissy Spacek was nominated five times (one award) over eleven years in the most sterile period in the history of film, as far as women's roles go. Through choosing her roles carefully and the directors with whom she has worked, Spacek has demonstrated her personal skills and talents and turned the characters she has played into first-rate performances.

Which is not the same as saying she is a "movie star." On the contrary, Spacek has carefully avoided the big star buildup and image, sublimating her own personality to the demands of the characters she plays. Instead, she has selected roles that displayed and increased her stature as an "actress."

She shares her power with her husband, Jack Fisk, whom she met on the set of *Badlands*. Spacek agreed to appear in Texan Bill Wittliff's film *Raggedy Man* in 1981, but only if Fisk were allowed to direct it. The film became his first directorial assignment; all of his previous film experience was as art director.

Spacek's 1986 films present a solid capsule of what she is about. The first film released, *Violets Are Blue*, was directed once again by Jack Fisk. Despite playing a dramatically appealing role, the film received lackluster reviews, as had *Raggedy Man*. The second film was a two-woman tour de force starring Spacek and Anne Bancroft in the cinematic adaptation of the Pulitzer Prize-winning play *'night Mother*. It was a downbeat story dealing with suicide that Spacek took on as a personal challenge. The third film, *Crimes of the Heart,* a black humorous gothic tale, was successful not only with the critics but also with audiences.

Thus, the three faces of Sissy Spacek: one turned toward her husband, one exclusively toward art, and the third toward art and audience. It takes a consumately talented artist to satisfy all three constituencies. To even a casual observer, it is apparent the freckle-faced veteran from Quitman knows how to act, and equally important, how to choose the roles she performs.

"If I'm going to tie my life to a character, she has to have something I really believe in," says Spacek. "There has to be something I can latch onto — some sort of social value, some sense of optimism, something that makes it worth turning myself inside out."

She has successfully resisted the best efforts of publicity agents to turn her into a "city slicker" and leave Texas and all that behind.

"Texas is the place that keeps me most grounded," she said. "When I get real nuts, I can go back there and walk in the woods and swim and water ski and go riding. . . . It's great."

It is quite likely that Sissy Spacek is in the early stage of the most successful cinematic career of any actress in American film history. But in spite of her huge film acclaim, she is also a woman whose consciousness is firmly rooted in familial values that transcend fame and public adulation. She acquired those standards in Quitman, Texas, and takes them with her, wherever she goes.

Sissy Spacek's professional debt to actors Rip Torn and Geraldine Page is incalculable. They both served as mentors to the younger Texan, and their influence can be seen not only in the roles Spacek has chosen, but also the style in which she plays them.

Torn and Page, both "method" actors closely associated with Actors Studio in New York, encouraged Sissy to study under Lee Strasberg at his Theatrical Institute after she had been in New York awhile. Spacek quit after six or eight months, saying, "I learned more walking from my apartment on 19th Street across 14th to Lee Strasberg's than I did in class. . . . I was working, really, before I knew exactly what I was doing." What helped her most were the techniques she learned from her cousin and his wife.

Elmore "Rip" Torn did not initially set out to become an actor. He majored in agriculture at Texas A&M for a year, then transferred to The University of Texas as an architecture student. Soon, however, he switched to the school of drama and earned his degree in that subject. As soon as he graduated, he hot-footed it to Hollywood to be discovered, but no producers found him in the kitchens where he cooked and washed dishes to earn his living. Deciding he needed more seasoning, Rip went back to Texas and became an apprentice at the Dallas Institute of Performing Arts. Baruch Lumet, father of film director Sidney Lumet, was in charge of the institute, and he had Rip plastering, painting flats, laying floors, and typing, as well as appearing in a few scenes.

At the height of the conflict in the Korean War, Torn enlisted in the army and served two years as a military policeman. When he was discharged in 1955, he headed straight for New York, where he was "discovered" by Elia Kazan, founder of the Actors Studio. Kazan guaranteed he could make Rip into another Brando or James Dean, two of his earlier protégés. Indeed, he gave Torn his first Broadway role as an understudy in *Cat on a Hot Tin Roof*. A month before the end of the show's long run, Rip got to play the role of Brick. From there he went into a series of prestigious live television programs that reads like a list of television's Golden Age teleplays. He also periodically flew to Hollywood for appearances in filmed TV shows, and in 1957 began his theatrical film career in *Time Limit*.

Meanwhile, Torn kept alive his ties to the theater by appearing in at least one stage play per year. He worked with Kazan on Broadway and in the lesser lights of Off-Broadway. Torn deliberately chose offbeat roles. However, beginning in 1962 with his appearance opposite Tuesday Weld in a "Naked City" episode, Torn had a decade ahead in which he would be typecast in TV shows only as a heavy. Film directors began to call for the Texan when they needed someone to portray villains and madmen, roles Torn felt he already had played too many times.

On the rare occasions Rip was given the opportunity, he proved he had a fine flair for comedy, first in *Critic's Choice* (1963), then in Francis Ford Coppola's *You're a Big Boy Now* (1967), in which he appeared with Geraldine Page. When he played the Henry Miller role in *Tropic of Cancer* (1970), *New York Times* movie critic Howard Thompson praised Torn's interpretation of Miller as "a brilliantly right personification." More recently, Torn's comedic talent has shown in such films as *Flashpoint*, starring Kris Kristofferson, and *Songwriter*, with Willie Nelson and Kristofferson.

Critical reactions to Torn's work have swung from one pole to the other, frequently in a very short span of time. For example, he appeared with George C. Scott and Colleen Dewhurst in an Off-Broadway revival of Eugene O'Neill's *Desire Under the Elms*. Of his interpretation of the character Eben Cabot, one critic said he acted "like a refugee from a Texas lunatic asylum." Only four months later, he received praise for "a sensitive and beautifully modulated performance" in another O'Neill play, *Strange Interlude*. A role in the Actors Studio Theater's Broadway production of *Blues for Mr. Charlie* led most critics to claim that Torn was "perfect."

But by the end of the sixties, every interviewer who talked to the Texan wanted to know why his Hollywood and theatrical career had foundered. There was no question but that it had. He had not become the big star Kazan had promised, and he frequently worked Off-Broadway, if he was to work at all. Furthermore, the roles he did get in television and films did not serve the forward thrust of his career. Rip Torn, an actor who had had such impressive credentials early in his career, was virtually dead in the water.

In an interview with Joseph Gelmis of *Newsday* (November 10, 1969), Torn suggested the existence of conspiracies, intrigue, and outright persecution as the causes for his stunted career. He even insisted that the driver of an automobile with which his motorcycle collided in New York City was "out to get" him. He told *New York Times* critic Mel Gussow that reports from Hollywood and Broadway of his temperamental behavior were false — or at least greatly exaggerated. That he was as surly, unstable, erratic, and violent as the stock-in-trade characters he portrayed, Torn flatly denied.

But the denial didn't explain why the Texan verifiably attacked Norman Mailer with a claw hammer during the filming of Mailer's improvised film, *Maidstone*. Torn has said that "every good actor is neurotic, difficult, crazy, or drunk."

Some have described the actor as his own worst enemy. But whatever the causes of the friction between Torn and Hollywood and Broadway during the sixties, his roles during the seventies and eighties have shown an ever-expanding range, from Shakespeare to dialect roles to comedy. He has gained new respect for his talent and ability as an actor. Even the Hollywood Establishment, which had regarded him as an outlaw for so long, was pleased to recognize his skill in 1984 with the nomination for Best Supporting Actor for his creation of the character of Marsh Turner, a Southern backwoodsman, in *Cross Creek*. Belated recognition by the Academy of Motion Picture Arts and Sciences, but welcome all the same.

Horton Foote has one of the least-recognized names of just about any major practitioner of film art from Texas. One reason for that is the Wharton native's low-key method of operating. Another is the division of his efforts between the New York stage, television, and Hollywood movies. But perhaps the main reason lies in his withdrawal from the movie scene for a full decade because he didn't like the direction things were going.

After graduating from Wharton High School in the middle thirties, Foote went west to become an actor. He apprenticed at the famous Pasadena Playhouse for a year, then went to New York to study under Tamara Daykarhanova, protégeé of Stanislavsky, founder of "the method" for actors. For the next few years, Foote worked as an actor, then began writing plays especially for production by the American Actors Theatre, a repertory troupe organized by Mary Hunter, who also had been a student of Daykarhanova. Lucy Kroll, another of the group, now serves as Foote's agent. As part of their rehearsals, members were encouraged to plumb the depths of their own regional diversity before pooling the results to arrive at the meaning of "American."

The sessions inspired Foote to delve into his Texan background for material, a direction he has followed since 1940 in his writings. He became a prolific writer and has composed eighteen stage dramas (mostly one-act plays), twenty or more teleplays, and more than a dozen screenplays, most of them adaptations of his own work, but a few from that of others. "From the beginning," he says, "most of my plays have taken place in the imaginary town of Harrison, Texas."

Foote won his first Oscar for his screenplay adapted from Harper Lee's novel *To Kill a Mockingbird* in 1962. Foote's next screenplay was called *Baby, the Rain Must Fall,* which he adapted from his play *The Travelling Lady.* In the film, a parolee rejoins his wife and daughter in a Southern town, but his violent outbursts split them apart again. A good cast, headed by Steve McQueen, Lee Remick, and Don Murray, plus hard work by everyone else, failed to produce an interesting film.

Foote's next movie, *The Chase*, was adapted from his novel of the same name. Playwright Lillian Hellman wrote the screenplay, but Foote edited the final version. In the movie, a convict escapes prison and heads home to a small Texas town. Every inhabitant of the community is affected one way or the other. Expensively filmed in 1966 by director Arthur Penn, the film turned into a shoddy essay of sex and violence in Texas rather than Peyton Place. Even Marlon Brando, Jane Fonda, Robert Redford, Robert Duvall, and others in the sterling cast could not pull it out. Texan critic Rex Reed called it, "The worst thing that has happened to movies since Lassie played a war veteran with amnesia." Philip T. Hartung said, "Considering all the talent connected with it, it is hard to imagine how *The Chase* went so haywire."

But the film that finally drove Foote to semi-retirement at his New Hampshire farm was one in which not a single word of his was used, though he was given co-scriptwriting credit. *Hurry Sundown*, produced in 1967, was a cliché-ridden epic melodrama, with action and sexual digressions, about racial problems in the Georgia farmlands. Jane Fonda and Michael Caine starred in the ill-fated effort, and Faye Dunaway was featured. Rex Reed came at the movie with six-guns blazing: "Critic Wilfrid Sheed wrote recently that no film is ever so bad that you can't find some virtue in it. He must not have seen *Hurry Sundown*." Wilfrid Sheed said of the film: "To criticize it would be like tripping a dwarf."

While writing "The Orphan's Home" plays at his New Hampshire hideaway, Foote was interrupted by old friend Robert Duvall's request for a screenplay. Foote responded with the gentle tale of a down-and-out country-western singer. It was called *Tender Mercies* (1983). Duvall plays Mac Sledge, the famous singer whose affinity for alcohol has dissolved career and marriage. He finds redemption in a small Texas town through the "tender mercies" of God and a new family. Fort Worth native Betty Buckley played his ex-wife, and Dallas-based Tess Harper his new one. A few critics found the story "ponderous" and "wearisome," but they were a distinct minority. Most liked it for its simplicity and subtlety.

"He has had fluctuating success in the theatre, film, and television," wrote Stanley Kauffman in the *New Republic*, "but his new screenplay is a beauty." Duvall said of Foote's writing, "You can't push it . . . you have to just let it lay there. It's like rural Chekhov, simple but deep." The screenplay won Foote his second Oscar, and Robert Duvall received the Best Actor award.

Meanwhile, Herbert Berghof began producing some of the "Orphan" plays at his H B Playhouse in Manhattan in 1982. Hallie, Foote's daughter, was then studying acting with a Berghof protégée at the Loft Studio in Los Angeles. She encouraged her father to translate the plays to the screen, which he has proceeded to do with the family's involvement. The first to reach the screen was *1918* (1985), produced by Lillian Foote, Horton's wife, and Ross Milloy. The film was directed by Ken Harrison of Dallas and starred Hallie Foote. Another daughter, Daisy, and son Horton, Jr., worked as production assistants. Horton, Jr. also had a supporting role in the film.

1918 recreates a story of family survival at the conclusion of World War I when an influenza epidemic raced across the world, killing as many people as had perished in the war. One critic complained of "unrelieved melancholy." More typical was the evaluation of David Sterritt of the *Christian Science Monitor:* "While it lacks the brilliance of *Tender Mercies,* it [*1918*] has a quiet manner and warm sensibility that make it a worthy successor to the earlier movie. In both pictures, Foote's approach is so delicate that it makes some viewers nervous. You keep waiting for something to happen, they complain, and it never does."

Time magazine's critic, Richard Corliss, calls *1918* "a home-movie reverie about people who are cordial but not awfully forthcoming . . . which is why *1918* has the effect of a ninety-one minute convalescence from the electroshock therapy of current Hollywood filmmaking."

The second film in the project was *On Valentine's Day* (1986), again featuring the Foote family with their contributions on and off the screen. Foote himself functions as co-director once more with Ken Harrison, though not for credit. That led some critics to assert that Foote's too-tight control is evident in the final product. Others thought the film "a labor of love" and "a thoughtful and literate drama" that stressed character and language over splashy film images and slick editing.

Both films were made for slightly over $1.5 million each — real shoestring budgets nowadays.

Foote's third Oscar nomination was for his 1985 script adapted from his play *The Trip to Bountiful.* When the play first was performed in 1953, Lillian Gish starred. She also played the lead in the teleplay of the story. In 1985 Geraldine Page gave a one-woman tour de force in the film, good enough to win the Oscar for Best Actress that year, though Foote's script did not win.

Blind Date, a one-act play, premiered Off-Broadway in May 1986. Frank Rich of the *New York Times* called it "a gem," adding that Foote "seems to rejuvenate himself with every passing year." PBS has presented Foote's adaptations of Faulkner's *Barn Burning* and Flannery O'Connor's *The Displaced Person*, and plans to air *The Story of a Marriage*. The latter will contain a filmed version of Foote's play *Courtship*, plus *On Valentine's Day* and *1918*. Several other Foote plays are in the works for production, and his most recently completed screenplay is *The Land of the Astronauts*.

Although Foote and his wife live in Manhattan, they make regular visits to Wharton. Several years ago, Foote bought the family house near downtown Wharton, refurbished it, and stays there on trips home. He has bought the last remaining plot in the Wharton cemetery.

The Texan told an interviewer for *New York Times Magazine* in 1986: "I believe deeply in the human spirit, and I have an awe about it, because I don't know how people carry on [in extremely difficult times]. . . . I'm always measuring myself. Could I do that? Could I take that?"

Anyone familiar with the body of Foote's work knows the answer to those questions. He has already proven himself, as a man and as an artist. He continues to do so with each new work, even now, in his eighth decade.

Farrah Fawcett may be the first woman who started her professional career as a model and "poster girl" to become recognized as a serious contender for Best Actress honors. Back in 1976, with a few television and movie roles to her credit, Fawcett posed for the poster shot in a wet, skin-tight, one-piece maillot bathing suit. That same year she played one of three major female roles in "Charlie's Angels," along with Texan Jaclyn Smith. The show stayed in the top-ten ratings week after week and ended the season as the number-one TV show in the country. Before long, given that weekly showcase, sales of the poster exceeded 8 million, at $2 to $3 a lick. Fawcett's poster sales demolished the previous record set by Marilyn Monroe.

"Charlie's Angels" featured good-looking women wearing

glamorous clothes who occasionally used guns to work their will as cops. It was popular with men, who watched the girls, and women, who watched the clothes. It was the original, prime-time "girlie" show. The *Los Angeles Times* critic observed that the show "drips with sexuality" and presents "good-natured but quite intentional teasing." *Time*'s reviewer said the series was "family-style porn, a mild erotic fantasy."

"It is the illuminated evanescence of Farrah Fawcett-Majors that is largely responsible for the success of 'Charlie's Angels,' " wrote Tom Shales in the *Washington Post.* "People must be turning in just to watch Farrah bounce around." Fawcett herself said, "I think people want to see some glamour, some clothes, some hair styles, you know — they want to see girls." Jay Bernstein, Farrah's manager at the time, summed up his client's appeal in the poster and in the show in one word: "Nipples."

Bernstein's assessment may be simplistic, or it may be simply accurate. For when Farrah quit the show after the first season, a studio executive is said to have described her replacement as follows: "[She] must, of course, be another well-stacked blonde with good bod and great looking legs, who can wear a T-shirt well and read four lines of dialogue off an idiot card." Farrah's replacement was Cheryl Ladd.

Some observers attributed Fawcett's departure to marital strain, although her contract guaranteed she could leave the set in time to get home and cook husband Lee Majors's supper. Much as she loved Lee and cooking, because of the heavy shooting schedule, public appearances, and demands on her time as the star of a top-rated TV show, Farrah finally told Lee: "If you want me in the bedroom, you'll have to hire somebody to do the dishes." It is also possible that Lee wanted to be the only star in the family, and Farrah's success was too threatening.

Her sudden fame brought her a $4.5 million endorsement for Faberge, a cool million for three hours of photo taking to plug a faucet-shaped necklace, and additional revenue from T-shirts, dolls, and lunch pails. Former agent-manager Bernstein said he refused a million-dollar offer from an enterprise wanting to merchandise bottled water "from Farrah's own faucet." The $5,000 per episode she got from "Angels" was like a paycheck for advertising herself. In four years, she made about $17 million.

With a solid financial base as a launching pad, Farrah set out to become a "serious" actress in theatrical films. Her first, shot in 1977, was called *Somebody Killed Her Husband*, and it was not kindly received by critics. *Time*'s reviewer was typical: "To buy this film's plot, it isn't enough to suspend disbelief; you have to submit to a lobotomy." Several other films of equal caliber followed: *Sunburn, Strictly Business, The Helper* (all in 1979), *Saturn 3* (1980), and *Cannonball Run* (1981).

A breakthrough came in 1981 with a made-for-TV film called *Murder In Texas*, for which Fawcett received high critical marks. Then, as have so many other actresses who want to prove themselves good at their profession, she went to New York to appear in an Off-Broadway production of a play called *Extremities*. The play also was well-received, and Fawcett later starred in the movie adapted from the play. Meantime, she scored with another television movie, *The Burning Bed*. In 1986 she played the part of a Nazi hunter in *The Beate Klarsfeld Story* for television. The Foreign Correspondents Association nominated her for Golden Globe awards as best dramatic actress in television for the *Klarsfeld Story* and best dramatic actress in a theatrical film for *Extremities*. Although she didn't win either award, being nominated marked a tremendous professional leap for the Corpus Christi native.

After nearly two decades in Hollywood, she was starting to get the kind of recognition she craved. Farrah had moved a considerable distance since her first TV appearance in Larry Hagman's "I Dream of Jeannie" series, where she had this unforgettable dialogue: "I have to change," she said. "Don't change too much," he said.

At age forty, Farrah has been married to only one man, actor Lee Majors. That marriage lasted from 1973 until 1982. Lee was an established actor when they met, and Farrah's acting prospects picked up when she met Majors. It wasn't until after her divorce that she realized her desire for freedom and independence. She once said, "I was always protected by my family. I liked being protected. It kept me from getting too wise too soon."

That may be so. She was certainly out of step with most of her peers at The University of Texas back in the sixties. A classmate observed that "She stood out like a painted pony, with her beauty and those clothes. . . . She looked like she just stepped out of a bandbox, and the rest of us were hanging around in beat-up jeans and sweatshirts. We were marching for peace, and Farrah was sitting there, smiling, and looking pretty. . . . We were experimenting with sexual freedom, and a little bit of dope. And Farrah, of course, would have none of that."

Farrah claimed to be happier after the divorce than she had ever been. Finally, she felt in control of her life. "Every woman needs to feel this kind of strength and independence *before* she gets into a relationship."

The words have a faintly ironic ring, inasmuch as she had taken up with Ryan O'Neal long before divorcing Majors. Though they are not married after nearly seven years together, they might as well be. They have a three-year-old son now, named Redmond.

Fawcett's acting career has reached new heights since her association with O'Neal. But it would be a logical fallacy to attribute her success to O'Neal, simply because it came after they began sharing lives.

Farrah has never pretended to be an intellectual heavyweight, but that is not a prerequisite for great success in films. What she has is a burning desire to prove she is more than just hair, teeth, and nice figure. With that kind of motivation, plus talent and a little luck, the scripts and directors will find her. It would come as no surprise if Farrah Fawcett wins the Oscar for Best Actress before she turns forty-five, despite the formidable competition she faces.

Gary Busey, from Goose Creek, found instant stardom playing the title role in *The Buddy Holly Story* in 1978; he even received an Oscar nomination. Then, for the next seven years, he wallowed in a deep career trough, primarily because of his love affair with drugs. He had been a drummer in rock and roll bands long before he became a film star, so he wasn't exactly a drug virgin when he hit it big in the movies.

Gary Busey started in television and films in 1970, with minor roles in "Bonanza," "Gunsmoke," and "Baretta." After making *The Last American Hero* in 1972 with Jeff Bridges, a friend in Tulsa who hosted a TV show invited Busey to appear, and he became a regular for several months. Leon Russell lived in Tulsa at the time, and he asked Busey to go on tour with his band. Tired of television, he went.

After the tour, Busey captured the lead in a short-lived TV series called "Texas Wheelers." The show lasted long enough to deprive the Texan of a role in *Nashville,* one he wanted. But after "Wheelers" bit the dust, he got a number of more rewarding roles in *The Law, The Execution of Pvt. Slovick,* and *Blood Sport.* Then he made *A Star is Born* with Kristofferson and Streisand, and his film fortunes began to improve considerably with the role of a junkie in *Straight Time* and culminated in *The Buddy Holly Story.*

Busey had good reason farther down the road to recall Leon Russell's sage advice after *Straight Time.* "Teddy Jack [the name Busey uses as a drummer], watch out for them roles you play, 'cause they'll jump right into your real time." Sure enough, Busey's film career went downhill as he came to rely more and more on artificial stimulants to keep on keeping on. *Carny* and *Fooling Around* (1980) failed at the box office, as did the movie he made with Nelson, *Barbarosa* (1982).

By the time he made *Bear* in 1984, Busey seriously needed a hit in a big way. He put a lot of time in, preparing for his portrayal of the great Alabama football coach Bear Bryant. He reminisced for seven months with Bear fans, watched 100 hours of videotapes of Bryant, and visited with the coach's family. The family didn't like the script, however, and they didn't want Busey playing the role. Filming went ahead anyway, and problems with Busey abounded. He exhibited a lot of paranoia and insecurity, and threw numerous temper tantrums. He pounded dents in the body of a rental car with his fists, merely because he had been booked in the tourist section for a flight back to Los Angeles. Rumors circulated freely that Busey was on drugs.

"No," said director Richard Sarafian. "Being clean is part of the contract." But Busey's behavior was more convincing to the cast and crew than Sarafian's statement.

It was another year before the Texan came up for air. His weight had ballooned to 240 ("all those donuts on the set") and, while he still got TV offers and an occasional movie, they weren't the kinds of things he wanted to do. When he finally got straight, he dropped sixty pounds and started getting good roles once more.

In 1986 and early 1987, he received salutary reviews for *Let's Get Harry,* in which he appeared with Robert Duvall; *The Eye of the Tiger,* directed by Richard Sarafian, in which he starred; and *Lethal Force,* opposite Mel Gibson and Danny Glover. He also was offered a starring role in the new TV series "Houston

Knights,'' but turned it down. He wants to make theatrical films, and lots of them.

Busey still has ability that is recognized by producers, and he has a solid opportunity to play the role that should guarantee the award he so desperately desires. If he keeps clean, his reach will surely not exceed his grasp.

The period of influential, serious stars did not escape directors. A couple of Texan directors had solidified their excellent careers long ago.

Josh Logan traveled from Texarkana, his birthplace, to Hollywood in the 1930s. He had organized the University Players, a summer stock group drawing most of its members from Princeton University, where Logan was an undergraduate. James Stewart, Henry Fonda, and Margaret Sullavan furthered their acting careers through the Players, and Logan became a recognized director with the group.

Later, he and Mary Martin were associated with some of the longest-running hits on the legitimate stage, including *South Pacific*. Martin's son, Larry Hagman, also appeared in one of Logan's stage productions.

As a movie director, Josh Logan became known as a sensitive, kind, caring helmsman who could get outstanding performances from stars as diverse as Marlon Brando and Marilyn Monroe.

The career of legendary director John Huston is a phenomenal one, and its roots were in Texas. Although born in Missouri, Huston established most of his childhood recollections in Weatherford, Texas, where his family had moved to when he was very young.

"My first memories are of Weatherford: being in the saddle in front of my mother at night, mesmerized by the sound of the horse's hooves striking cobblestones.

"My childhood memories of Weatherford are pleasant, but it was there my parents' marriage began to fall apart. Dad was doing his best to be a good husband and father, but he was a born actor and couldn't get it out of his system," Huston remembered.

John's Texas grandmother read to him frequently throughout his childhood. One of his favorite Weatherford pieces was a lengthy poem titled "Yankee Doodle Dandy." He asked her to read it often, and one day when her glasses had been misplaced, John recited the verses. All forty-eight of them.

It wasn't long afterward that he made his first "professional" appearance. He still remembers the announcer's introduction on the stage in Dallas: "Forty-eight verses . . . and only three years and seven months old. . . ." John Huston's love affair with show business started in Texas that evening. He continued to appear on stages around Weatherford through first grade, when he and his divorced mother moved away. But he wasn't through with Texas, or Texas women. One of the women he married was the Port Arthur actress who played Scarlett O'Hara's sister in *Gone With the Wind,* Evelyn Keyes.

Potentially one of the most commanding directors in Hollywood today is Terrence Malick from Waco. Son of an oil company executive, Malick spent much of his youth in the Panhandle. During summers, like many Texas teenage boys, he worked the wheat harvests all the way up into Canada. Then his father sent him to Harvard, and later to Oxford as a Rhodes Scholar. During the mid-sixties, Malick worked as a journalist for *Newsweek, Life,* and the *New Yorker.* Then he lectured in philosophy at MIT for a year before going to California to attend the American Film Institute for Advanced Film Studies. His output has been small but attention-getting.

Malick supported himself and his wife by rewriting scripts such as *Dirty Harry,* and as sole author of the script *Pocket Money* (1972), starring Paul Newman and Lee Marvin. It is the story of two cowboys who think they can earn money herding cattle. Although the peculiar Western comedy-drama appealed immensely to the participants who made it, the film was too offbeat to be a commercial success.

In 1973 Malick wrote, produced, and directed the haunting and provocative film about a young couple on a senseless killing spree in the Badlands of Dakota and Montana. *Badlands,* starring Martin Sheen and Sissy Spacek, was received enthusiastically by critics at the New York Film Festival, although Pauline Kael (Malick's former colleague at the *New Yorker*) thought it too cerebral. Jonathan Rosenbaum called it "one of the finest literate examples of narrated cinema since the early days of Welles and Polonsky." It quickly became a cult film and still maintains its reputation as a finely crafted movie.

Since *Badlands* made no money, Malick turned to his pen once again, pseudonymously writing a gangster movie called *The Dion Brothers* under the name David Whitney in 1974. Other hack work followed during the intervening four years until his next film appeared. *Days of Heaven* starred Richard Gere, Brooke Adams, Sam Shepard, and teenager Linda Manz in her first movie. The film shows, in breathtaking beauty, what it was like farming wheat in the Texas Panhandle early in the century — how the farmers lived, how the grasshoppers and wheat grains and combines looked, the changes wrought by the seasons. The plot is slight, on the surface, and seems to be merely an excuse for the visual images. But once more, critics loved the exacting mission Malick set for himself. They favorably compared the film with *The Grapes of Wrath*, one of the greatest pictures in the annals of Hollywood.

In preparation of his book *American Film Now* (1979), respected film historian James Monaco conducted a survey among what he considered the *world's* twenty best critics. The critics were asked to name the top ten films — no more nor less — released between January 1, 1968, through December 31, 1977. The top seven films selected were made by the most celebrated directors of the second half of the twentieth century. Number eight on the list was Terrence Malick's *Badlands*. It would have been especially interesting to know how Malick would have ranked had the survey been extended one year to include his *Days of Heaven*.

The sad part of Malick's story is the same as that of any other artist who attempts great art: the audience for art is so small, especially in a mass medium, that the artist cannot earn a living at it. Malick has been busy since 1978, but the fruits of his efforts have been small. Nobody wants to put money into a film destined for commercial failure.

Today he makes very few public appearances and says even less about what he is doing. "*Taciturn* is the word for Terry," says a person who has worked with him. Studio biographies are brief, and Malick only grants interviews with the stipulation that he not be quoted. He is famous in Hollywood for being tight-lipped about his projects at all times, preferring to let the finished work speak for itself. Perhaps he is now busy at work on his *magnus opus*. It would be a pity if the philosopher has had his filmic say.

The second quickest way to the director's chair is through an apprenticeship as a screenwriter. Of the elements necessary to put together a film package, a star outranks the script in most cases, but a good writer has a way of attracting big stars and directors and, as a consequence, the money to finance the film.

Robert Benton, a Waxahachie native, and David Newman were the two most famous screenwriters of the sixties. They met at *Esquire* magazine, where Benton worked as a writer, then art director, and Newman was an editor. In 1966 they teamed up to write the Broadway play *It's a Bird . . . It's a Plane . . . It's Superman*. The following year they made a splashy entry into filmmaking with the script for *Bonnie and Clyde*. The film elicited eight nominations for Academy Awards and won two Oscars. Benton and Newman were nominated for the script. Critic Alexander Walker prophetically noted that it was "a film from which we shall date reputations and innovations in American cinema." The pair's next project was the Off-Broadway production, *Oh! Calcutta!* They eventually did the screen version as well. Benton and Newman produced the script for *There Was a Crooked Man*, starring Henry Fonda and Kirk Douglas, in 1970.

Benton made his directorial debut in the successful *Bad Company* (1972) from a script he and Newman wrote. His next outing as director was in a major film of 1977, *The Late Show*, from his own script, and produced by Robert Altman. After collaborating on the *Superman* film script, Benton once again assumed the director's mantle and became the top seed in Hollywood.

His popularity mushroomed with a late seventies hit. Nothing could withstand the magnitude of devotion to *Kramer vs. Kramer* at the 1979 Academy Awards. The topic of divorce had little inherent appeal to the 15–24 age bracket that filmmakers usually aim for, but the film did draw the interest of Academy members who vote for Oscar winners. Perhaps two-thirds of the voting members were intimately familiar with the subject. The film relied on old-fashioned film structure and solid performances by Dustin Hoffman and Meryl Streep, who both took Oscars. Benton received Oscars for directing and screenwriting. As a capstone, the film was chosen Best Picture of the Year, which added another $25 million to its gross receipts. If there was any doubt as to Benton's authorial or directorial talents, they were erased completely that night.

In 1984 Benton returned to his childhood home and memories

with *Places in the Heart.* The story is not unlike one of the numerous sentimental silent films which derived from nineteenth-century theatrical melodrama. The Texan doesn't claim to be an innovator, he merely uses things that have worked cinematically in the past to construct his modern films.

Places in the Heart is a simple story of a widow trying to save the farm and keep her family together after her sheriff husband gets killed. The film opens with a montage of grace-saying families as they eat Sunday dinner after church. The film ends in a church fantasy that unifies disparate elements of the town in a state of grace. At the beginning, a family is on the verge of disintegration and undergoes trials and tribulations that test the human spirit. By the end, the family has reformed, incorporating a blind man and a black man, and faces the future with a quiet optimism.

The film received a slew of Oscar nominations, but only Sally Field won an award as Best Actress. By coincidence, Benton's film was one of three major movies that year which centered on hard-pressed families fighting to save their farms. The others were *Country*, with Jessica Lange, and *The River*, starring Sissy Spacek. *Time*'s reviewer said, however, that "neither [of the other films] is informed by Benton's compulsion to sort out what matters from what merely seems to matter in a living memory's core. It is the patient care with which he addressed that problem, and the example he obviously set for his colleagues, that will permit his film to find its place in many a heart this season."

In another year, *Places in the Heart* would have won more Oscars. *Newsweek*'s critic Jack Kroll called *Places* "a beautifully controlled dream that fills reality with sweetness without falsifying it."

But just as Benton's *Kramer* could not be stopped in 1979, *Amadeus* rolled over all opposition in 1985. The film took eight Oscars altogether, including Best Actor for F. Murray Abraham, who studied at the University of Texas at El Paso.

There are numerous other Texans who have demonstrative grounds for being subjects of this chapter. And more of them are becoming involved in film production on both sides of the camera, which should elevate the chances for artistic success attributable to Lone Star natives in the future. As it stands now, a pretty fair crop is operating in Eden. And with luck, they will survive the bite of the apple.

No Memory of Having Starred
Keeps the End
From Being Hard

Perhaps one of the most significant attributes of Texan stars is that many still are imbued with the same frontier spirit that led their forefathers/mothers to leave the East for Texas. The faint of heart mostly stay home and rarely achieve greatly, especially in risky endeavors such as the movies, which have been a crapshoot from the beginning. But Texans seem to have an abundance of the gambler's instinct and confidence in their ability to do what they set out to accomplish. Drawn west by the exciting medium of film, their actions are completely consistent with their heritage.

Natives of the Lone Star State are accustomed to adversity, have grown up with it, and do not fear it. In fact, many have been attracted to Hollywood because of the very challenge it offered. Sometimes it was the provocation of a difficult feat, the same kind of attraction that had brought their forefathers to the dangerous, untamed wilds of Texas in the first place. Those who went to Hollywood simply carried on a family tradition. They were used to meeting and overcoming obstacles, and took pride in themselves for doing it.

Studies by psychologists show that the character trait most essential for success in Hollywood or in any demanding field is perseverance. What if King Vidor had decided to write only fifty scenarios before giving up, when after just two more, he made the breakthrough that encouraged him to continue writing screenplays? Or if Willie Nelson, after the poor stepchild treatment he had received in Nashville in the sixties, had determined to chuck his performing career and do something else? Example after example could be cited of Texans who would not give up, who refused to cave in under the most difficult circumstances.

Living on the frontier meant developing one's imaginative skills, for there were few external sources of diversion or entertainment. Mostly products of a society steeped in an oral tradition, the Texans relied heavily on their capacity to translate sounds into visual imagery. Skills developed along this line served them well in Hollywood. Anyone who cannot imagine performing successfully in an activity is unlikely to pursue it.

Given the frontier mentality most Texans have grown up with, whether in the age of cattle, oil, or space, the movie industry was made to order. The men who became film moguls all started in their twenties or early thirties. As a completely new business enterprise, few older, more conservative men were inclined to invest much in the future of the movies, in either time or money. Likewise, it is rare for older people to live on the edge of the frontier; they have too much to lose. It takes energy, ambition, and a willingness to risk everything on success, to try new directions. Texas produced plenty of young people who were willing and able to do it.

As a whole, Texans have not placed much stock in precedents or connections to get ahead. Naturally, as the state's society has matured, that has become less the case. But there is not one familial dynasty in filmmaking that had its origins in Texas. True, there have been a few families where several members worked in films, but nothing on the order of the Selznicks, Fondas, Douglases, or others. Texans generally exhibit too much pride to rely on a relative to grease the skids for them, preferring instead to make it on their own. Had they originated in an older cultural setting familiar with the obstacles, they might have been dissuaded from even attempting Hollywood. Because the film business is rife with nepotism and closed networks, perhaps more than any other industry in the United States, and newcomers without linkages who get a break are considered flukes.

"Independent" may be the word that best characterizes those Texans who made a success in films. Never ones to follow the herd, they insisted on being their own persons. And individualism is what makes one a star, whether as actor, writer, director, producer, couturier, or art director. Those who imitate always come out second or fifth best, if at all. Jayne Mansfield could not out-Monroe Monroe, and her flame flickered and went out when she proved unable to rid herself of the obsession to be like Marilyn. But when one thinks of Joan Crawford, Ginger Rogers, or Sissy Spacek, it is clear they *were* the creators of their original, distinct screen personas. They weren't trying to be another *anybody,* only exceptionally good at their craft.

Basically, the successful Texans in Hollywood had the courage to be what they chose to be, the courage to persevere when virtually every element seemed to be against them. Gene Autry had no acting skills at all when he arrived in Hollywood. The studio decided he needed diction lessons, and in his next film, Gene spoke his lines as if he had just come from class. Despite knowing that he would never be much of an actor or singer or rider, the Texan kept going, eventually winning great public acceptance and financial rewards. He exhibited the courage to face unknown challenges and had the tenacity to stick to his guns when unscrupulous producers tried to keep him down. He fought for his convictions, and he won.

Underpinning all these qualities is the bedrock emotional honesty displayed by Texans winning in Eden. Nothing is phonier or more obvious than "acting" in films. The medium is too intimate, too close; it sees too clearly and reveals too much.

There is a "staginess" about Broadway actors. That is, they must use larger-than-life gestures and intonations so they can be seen and heard in the last row of the balcony. Audiences accept the overplaying as one of the conventions of the theater and give it no further thought or consideration. Film, on the other hand, reveals even the faintest tremor of lip or flicker of eyelid, amplifies the tiniest catch in voice or breathing, shows the effects of thoughts on the face and body as clearly as one's hand before the eyes. Stage actors playing a role which may last two hours, eight times a week, week after week, necessarily must simulate emotion rather than feel it. Otherwise, they could not continue performing. Film actors, because of the microscopic nature of the camera, *must* feel the emotion; simulation would be recognized immediately and categorized as bad acting. But because film actors work such brief periods before the camera, this kind of acting does not leave them emotionally drained. To emit the appropriate feelings, film actors must possess emotional integrity, and Texans have shown more than a sufficient amount of that quality.

What was life like for Texans who had made a success in Hollywood?

Most people are familiar with the flamboyant lifestyles of some Hollywood artists. The life of Mary Pickford, First Lady of Hollywood, led her to her bed in Pickfair, sucking gin from the nipple of a baby bottle.

Writer-director-producer King Vidor partook of some of the temptations of Eden and avoided others. He married, fathered children, divorced several times, and had numerous romances. Long after he retired from filmmaking, Vidor remained very active socially in Hollywood and Beverly Hills until he died.

King Vidor was never known as a man who threw his money away foolishly, especially on drink or drugs. A strong Christian Scientist, he followed a healthful regime in his everyday life. In truth, Vidor could have lived in Dallas or Austin and been perfectly at home. Always handsome, Vidor was a favorite with women, especially actresses. As director, he exercised his *droit de seignior* to their charms. He believed actresses gave stronger performances if they were in love with their director. However, there is no evidence that Vidor ever abused his position.

Howard Hughes's record, as we have seen, was not quite as clean. The roles of professional and private transactions were virtually inseparable for Hughes. The few private satisfactions he had were almost inevitably linked to his "public" life; i.e., his work, as Howard was never a public figure in the same sense as other powerful, wealthy men. And after his plane crash in 1946, Hughes made even fewer appearances in public than before.

One example of the obsession with privacy that ruled Hughes's life, if another is needed, relates to Joseph L. Mankiewicz's film, *The Barefoot Contessa*. This instance also shows how effective was the smokescreen Howard Hughes contrived to conceal his real doings.

After Hughes finally broke off his relationship with Linda Darnell, she took up with writer-producer-director Joe Mankiewicz. Darnell claimed he wrote the screenplay for *Contessa* in her bedroom, that she read the script while he was writing it, and that the part of Maria Vargas (played by Ava Gardner) was supposed to be hers. Mankiewicz denied Darnell's account, but certain elements in one of the film's characters might have been conveyed to Mankiewicz by someone with Darnell's intimate knowledge of Howard Hughes.

In the shooting script are transparent references to Hughes that are undeniable. Harry Dawes (Humphrey Bogart) says: "That's what a man looks like whose grandfather made good, whose mother left him with two hundred million dollars, whose father ran away and hid from the world . . . poor little rich boy . . . His money came from a patent on a stamping machine [Hughes's came from an oil-well drilling bit his father patented] and his heart was a valve in a stamping machine. Why did Kirk Edwards want to produce movies? The answer is more simple than anyone thinks. Because he wanted girls."

His enormous wealth allowed Hughes not only to find seclusion in Hollywood; it also helped him to take control of women. One of the Hollywood legends surrounding Hughes is that he put Gina Lollobrigida under contract, then locked her away in a house. That may be accurate, or a variation on stories from numerous sources of Hughes signing young Hollywood starlets to personal contracts, then requiring them to be by their phones twenty-four hours a day in case he wished to speak with them. They were virtual prisoners in their apartments, for which he paid.

When Ava Gardner divorced Mickey Rooney in 1943, Hughes provided a safe hideaway for Ava so that she could avoid Rooney's importunities to come back home. During a quarrel with Hughes at the hideaway, Gardner knocked the lanky, six-foot-four-inch Texan out cold with an ashtray. In *Contessa,* Harry Dawes's voice again (he narrates much of the film as well as playing a major character in it): "Kirk didn't possess a home, really. He lived mainly in his office, and he maintained a half-dozen tiny apartments as hideaways. After all, his life was that of an alley cat — and he always had an available furnished alley to go to."

One of Hughes's lawyers was a Hollywood socialite, the handsome Greg Bautzer, something of an alley cat himself. After reading the script, he called Mankiewicz in New York.

"Joe, we've got to do something about this. Howard likes you, and it's a marvelous script, but you're cutting a little too close to the bone, and Howard doesn't like that."

Joe screened the film for the heads of United Artists and their libel attorney, Louis Nizer. Nizer cut to the point: "You had better listen to the man. He's got a case."

Mankiewicz went to Hollywood immediately and met with Hughes and Bautzer in Hughes's Beverly Hills bungalow hideaway. He denied that Hughes was the model for Edwards, but Hughes said others might not see it that way. To make the changes Hughes wanted was nearly impossible in view of the film's premiere performance set two weeks off, moaned Mankiewicz. The chief difficulties related to travel and distance. For Howard Hughes, no problems were insurmountable, especially these, because he owned Trans World Airways. Hughes provided letters to officers at all major airports involved in the travel. (For various technical reasons, the film editor had to go from New York to California to South America to London and back.) By the time he was finished, Kirk Edwards had metamorphosed from a Texas Tycoon to a Wall Street Lion.

There were those whose personalities became lost in the roles they played. The prime example is Joan Crawford.

Hollywood lawyer Greg Bautzer romanced Crawford longer than most of her marriages lasted, four years. The affair came to an end one night when Bautzer spoke with a young actress at a party while Crawford was occupied with someone else. On the way home, Joan, driving his car, asked Bautzer to check the right rear tire to see if it was low on air. It was 1:30 A.M. in a town that went to bed early. As Bautzer got out and bent over to check the tire, Crawford sped away, leaving Bautzer to walk to his suite at the Bel Air Hotel, several miles away. The roses she sent the next day didn't heal the wound she had caused by her high-handed behavior. But she was acting the part of the scorned lover.

Joe Mankiewicz had written a screenplay for Joan Crawford soon after he went to work for MGM. She liked not only what he had done with the script, she liked Joe, too, as did many Hollywood women. Before long they became lovers and good friends, as well as colleagues. Mankiewicz and Crawford made nine pictures together, with Joe producing eight of them himself. It was the most successful collaboration of Crawford's career. Louis Mayer, in assigning Joe to produce her films, exclaimed: "You're the only one who knows what to do with her!"

Mankiewicz was an acute observer of humankind, especially the female variety. Working so closely with Crawford over a period of years, he got to study her firsthand: "She woke up like a movie star, she went to the john like a movie star." In short, he said, she enjoyed playing Joan Crawford. Joe realized that, like many if not all actors, she was always playing a role. Unsure of her own identity, she tried on new guises to suit changing situations. If she was dressed to the teeth when she arrived at his office, Joe would ask his secretary to bring Miss Crawford a glass of sherry, and he would treat her formally and with courtly restraint. On the other hand, if she came waltzing in wearing slacks, he might pat her on the butt and ask, "Gettin' much, kid?" and give her a knowing wink.

As Crawford explained later, "I was trying to find myself. . . . I didn't know what I was or who I was. He knew that. That's why we got along together so well. He picked up on my moods. At the time I didn't realize it."

There is little to indicate that, armed with this knowledge, Joan Crawford changed much as she aged. The characters she played just got older.

Some of the Texas veterans, such as Ginger Rogers, survived relatively unscathed.

Rogers is still actively performing in 1987, on stage with a revival of *Babes in Arms*. Within her sixth decade in show business, Rogers appears to be indefatigable. But the highs of her long career have been reached, and after five childless marriages, none of which lasted very long, Ginger lives her life alone. Lela, her mother, confidante, guide, and lifelong best friend, died in Palm Springs in 1977.

If she were eighteen today and just starting out, would Ginger head for Hollywood again? Definitely not, she told an interviewer early in 1987. Contemporary films contain too much nudity, profanity, and emphasis on drugs. That is why she turns down so many roles, says Rogers, who is "shocked" by what she reads.

Asked if she gets lonely with no husband at home (she divorced the last one in 1961), she says: "I don't mind being alone.

Sometimes it's not easy. It'd be fun to have a chum around, but it's very hard to have a chum unless you're married to him, and I don't believe in today's concept of living with someone unmarried. . . . It's either marriage or be alone."

She misses not having a family, until she rethinks the matter. "Maybe I should be glad, because so many children got involved in drugs or went to jail or killed themselves. . . . Look at what Joan Crawford's daughter did to her with that book. . . . They wait until you die, and then they write a book saying horrible things about you."

Despite her regrets, she deemphasizes them; today is what counts, she figures. Her life, she says, had no conscious plan. She took it a step at a time, and that gave her a career. A deeply religious Christian Scientist, Rogers says the most important thing in her life is giving and receiving love.

The impact of Hollywood on an innocent soul can be studied in the life of a Texan hero, Audie Murphy.

Murphy's childhood, like Joan Crawford's, could serve as the model for a Charles Dickens or Erskine Caldwell novel. His parents were sharecroppers when he was born in 1924 outside of Kingston. One of nine children abandoned by his father when Audie was fifteen, he dropped out of school to help support his family by hunting rabbits with a borrowed .22 rifle. Since the barely surviving family could afford few cartridges, the future war hero sharpened his shooting eye to get a rabbit or squirrel with one shot.

When his mother died in 1941, Audie Murphy tried to enlist in the Marine Corps and paratroopers. He was rejected by both services because of his slight frame and frail body, brought about by years of undernourishment. He finally convinced older sister Corinne to falsify his birthdate so he could join the army. By the time he was eighteen, at his insistence, Murphy saw combat with the Third Infantry Division in Sicily and Italy. As the Allies fought their way north into France and Austria, Audie Murphy was in combat almost continually, earning a battlefield commission as an officer when he was twenty. At war's end, Murphy had won twenty-four citations for bravery, including the Silver Star and three Purple Heart medals. Officials estimated he had killed approximately 240 Germans in combat.

In one encounter, he held an outpost he had been ordered to defend to the end. With all his platoon dead or wounded, and wounded himself, he climbed atop a tank destroyer. Bleeding profusely from multiple wounds, the Texan turned his red-hot machine gun against the attacking Nazi force of 250 men and single-handedly repulsed the enemy. That exploit earned him the Medal of Honor.

Murphy was declared the most decorated soldier of World War II, and, in fact, he is the most decorated man in the history of American soldiery. He was a national hero when the army discharged him with a fifty percent disability pension due to his war injuries.

After the war, an airline stewardess named Pamela Archer sent his photograph to the Cagney brothers, William the producer, and James the actor. They offered him a shot at the movies in *Beyond Glory*, followed by *Texas, Brooklyn and Heaven*, both released in 1948. The next year Audie had his first starring role in *Bad Boy*, where he played an unconvincing juvenile delinquent.

Untrained as an actor, Murphy was extremely ill at ease in front of the camera. The few movies he made produced little income, and his entire pension went to support younger brothers and sisters in a Texas orphanage. Murphy was often obliged to sleep on the floor of a gymnasium owned by a friend.

In 1950 producers and directors got a handle on Murphy's persona when they starred him in *The Kid From Texas*, a box-office success. Universal put him on contract with plans to make him a big Western star. His autobiography, *To Hell and Back*, came out about this time, and the studio wanted to cash in on Audie's renewed fame as a war hero.

Director John Huston thought he could get a believable performance from the Texan as the young soldier in *The Red Badge of Courage*. The ex-soldier gave his best screen portrayal, but MGM politics caused the film to be so poorly edited it became a box-office flop.

Coming on top of a brief, failed marriage to actress Wanda Hendrix, Audie's private life in Hollywood was not much of a cut above that of combat in the war. Then he married the stewardess who got him started in Hollywood, Pam Archer, in 1951. It, too, was a stormy marriage.

After the MGM debacle, Murphy went back to Universal and

starred in two or three Westerns a year, usually as the traditional hero who faces difficult tasks, tough moral decisions, and dangerous enemies. He was always successful. His small stature and unexceptional good looks made Audie seem "ordinary," and filmgoers accepted him as completely believable. Frequently, the film hero merely wanted to live in peace rather than change the world or correct its wrongs. When he played Billy the Kid or Jesse James, Murphy still came across as the small-town boy who had fame thrust upon him.

Tony Curtis turned down the part of the Texan hero in the film version of *To Hell and Back,* so Audie played himself. It was his most commercially successful film, and by the end of the fifties, Audie Murphy was the top star of B-Westerns. He also began appearing on television at this time. In 1961 he starred for a season in NBC's "Whispering Smith" series, but for some reason, television was not his medium.

While the fifties for Murphy were professionally rewarding, the reverse proved true for the sixties. John Huston teamed up with Audie to make a psychological Western called *The Unforgiven,* but the movie didn't earn big money. Soon Murphy was back in the inexpensive adventure films at Universal.

The honesty of the Texan was disarming. "I'm working with a handicap," he declared. "I have no talent."

As his film career drew to a close near the end of the decade, he made an observation that would be repeated almost verbatim a few years later, with only slight modification, by Elvis Presley about his own film career. Murphy said, "I've made the same Western about forty times, only with different horses. I don't mind being an actor as long as I don't have to live up to a reputation I don't have."

Along with the demise of his Hollywood career came the disintegration of Murphy's personal life. He was deeply in debt, the $2.5 million he had earned lost in poor investments or given away. He was engulfed by bad publicity when police charged him with assault with intent to commit murder of a dog trainer, allegedly for beating a friend's dog. A jury acquitted him. He was separated from his second wife Pam, mother of his two children, Terry and James. It didn't seem as if things could get much worse.

On the evening of May 28, 1971, Murphy took off from Atlanta, Georgia, in a twin-engine Aero Commander to attend a business meeting he felt would mend his financial fences. The plane crashed outside Roanoke, Virginia. Audie Murphy was three weeks short of his forty-seventh birthday when he was buried in Arlington National Cemetery beside America's other greatest heroes.

Four years later, Murphy's widow and two sons received $2.5 million to settle a negligence suit filed against the pilot of the aircraft and the company that owned it. In one last, terrifying moment, the diminutive, brave Texan produced with his life the exact sum of money he had endured twenty years of Hollywood to earn.

Although death seems to many people the ultimate tragedy when it is untimely, as in Audie Murphy's case, it probably came as a blessing to him. One had only to see those troubled green eyes, looking out of a scarcely changing, boyishly handsome face, to know that an emotionally tortured soul lay behind them. From racking poverty unknown to present-day Americans, to instantaneous fame as a soldier-hero, Murphy came out of the war frightened and tormented by his experiences. Then came film popularity that he could not understand and with which he never learned to cope, in addition to the extensive exploitation by film executives.

Audie Murphy will never be known as a great film actor. He had a couple of chances to be quite good, but other factors interfered. Bad studio policy. Bad timing. Bad luck.

Which is about where we began this examination of Texans who went west to Eden. Few would deny that talent and personality play a part in Hollywood success, but from the mouths of babes comes the ultimate wisdom. Call it fate, karma, or destiny, but what it really takes is luck. Not talent. Not preparation. Not training or connections. Just luck.

The wheel of fortune goes round and round. Sometimes it stops while you are on top. At other times, on the bottom. Most of the time you are somewhere in between when you step off the wheel and out of Eden.

But in spite of the grief and heartache that frequently attend their sojourns to the West, few Texans would trade their lives in Hollywood for the ones led by their cousins who stayed at home. They are still frontiersmen and women in spirit, following the sun over one more hill.

Texans Who Went West to Eden

(Alphabetical Order)

Abraham, F. Murray. b. Pittsburgh, PA, 10-24-39. ed. UT-El Paso. Actor.

Ahearn, Thomas J. b. Dallas, 2-23-04. Writer.

Alexander, Richard. b. Dallas, 11-18-02. Actor.

Allen, Bob. b. Fort Worth. Actor.

Allen, Debbie. b. Houston. Actress, dancer.

Allen, Jacqueline. b. Texas. Attended schools Calvert, Waco, Houston. Actress.

Ames, Adrienne. b. Fort Worth, 8-3-09. d. 5-31-47. Actress.

Anderson, Andy. b. Arlington. Writer, director.

Andrews, Dana. b. Collins, MS, 1-1-09. Lived in Texas much of early life. ed. Sam
     Houston State. Actor.

Arledge, John. b. Crockett, 3-12-06. ed. UT. Actor.

Autry, Gene. b. Tioga, 9-29-07. Actor, singer, producer.

Avery, Fred (Tex). b. Dallas, 1907. d. 8-26-80. Animator.

Baker, Joe Don. b. Groesbeck, 2-12-36. Actor.

Banton, Travis. b. Waco, 8-18-94. Costume designer.

Barrett, Judith. b. Arlington, 2-2-14. Actress.

Barry, Donald (Red). b. Houston, 1-11-12. d. 1980. Actor, director.

Bates, Florence. b. San Antonio, 4-15-88. d. 1-31-54. Actress.

Bellamy, Madge. b. Hillsboro, 6-30-00. Actress.

Benson, Robby. b. Dallas, 1-21-56. Actor.

Benton, Robert. b. Waxahachie, 9-29-32. Director, screenwriter.

Blakely, Susan. b. Frankfort, Ger., 1950. ed. UT. Actress.

Blocker, Dan. b. Bowie County, 1929. d. 1972. Actor.

Boles, John. b. Greenville, 10-27-95. d. 2-27-69. Actor.

Bond, Tommy. b. Dallas, 9-16-27. Actor.

Boone, Pat (Charles Eugene). b. Jacksonville, FL, 6-1-34. Lived Fort Worth. ed.
     North Texas State. Actor, singer.

Boyd, Bill. b. Fannin County, 9-29-10. Actor, musician.

Boyd, William M. b. Shreveport, LA, 11-29-47. Actor, writer, musician.

Brian, Mary. b. Corsicana, 2-17-08. Actress.

Broaddus, Milton (Tex). b. Summerville, 9-16-27. Actor, dancer.

Brooks, Jean. b. Houston, 12-23-16. Actress.

Brown, James. b. Desdemona, 3-22-20. Actor.

Buchanan, Larry. b. Dallas. Director.

Buck, Frank. b. Gainesville, 3-17-88. d. 3-25-50. Producer, hunter, explorer.
Buckley, Betty. b. Fort Worth. Actress.
Buetel, Jack. b. Dallas, 9-5-17. Actor.
Burkley, Dennis. b. Grand Prairie. Actor.
Burnett, Carol. b. San Antonio, 4-26-33. Actress.
Burns, Marilyn. b. Austin. Actress.
Busey, Gary. b. Goose Creek, 6-29-44. Actor, musician.
Butts, Billy. b. Dallas, 9-8-19. Actor.
Camp, Joe. b. Dallas, 1940. Director, producer, screenwriter.
Capshaw, Kate. b. Fort Worth. Actress.
Carewe, Edwin. b. Gainesville, 3-5-83. d. 1-22-40. Director, producer.
Carson, Sunset. b. Plainview. 11-12-22. Actor.
Charisse, Cyd. b. Amarillo, 3-8-21. Dancer, actress.
Coleman, Dabney. b. Austin, 1-3-32. Actor.
Coleman, Ornette. b. Fort Worth. Actor, composer, musician.
Collins, Kathleen. b. San Antonio. Actress.
Comer, Anjanette. b. Dawson, 8-7-42. ed. Baylor. Actress.
Cooke, Ray. ed. San Antonio. Actor.
Crawford, Joan. b. San Antonio, 3-23-04. d. 1977. Actress.
Daniels, Bebe. b. Dallas, 1-14-01. d. 3-16-71. Actress.
Darnell, Linda. b. Dallas, 10-16-21. d. 1965. Actress.
Davis, Mac. b. Lubbock, 1-21-42. Actor, singer.
Dean, Eddie. b. Posey, 1910. Actor, singer.
Dean, Jimmy. b. Seth Ward, 8-28-28. Singer, actor.
Devore, Dorothy. b. Fort Worth, 1899. d. 1976. Actress.
Dexter, Elliott. b. Galveston, 1870. d. 1941. Actor.
Doran, Ann. b. Amarillo, 10-28-13. Actress.
Dover, Nancy. b. Arlington, 2-2-09. Actress.
Duncan, Sandy. b. Henderson, 2-20-46. Actress, singer.
Duncan, Tommy. b. Hillsboro, 1-11-11. Actor, musician.
Duvall, Shelley. b. Houston, 1949. Actress.
Early, Dudley. b. Paris, 1-18-03. Writer.
Easton, Robert. b. Milwaukee, WI, 11-23-30. ed. UT. Actor.
Ely, Ron. b. Hereford, 6-21-38. Actor.
Evans, Dale. b. Uvalde, 10-31-12. Actress, singer.
Fairchild, Morgan. b. Dallas, 2-3-50. Actress.
Fawcett, Farrah. b. Corpus Christi, 2-2-47. Actress.
Flowers, Bess. b. Sherman, 1900. Actress.
Foote, Hallie. Daughter Horton. Actress.
Foote, Horton. b. Wharton, 3-14-16. Writer.
Forman, Tom. b. West Texas, ca. 1894. Director.
Forrest, Steve. b. Huntsville, 9-29-24. Actor.
Fox, Wallace. b. Purcell, OK, 3-9-95. ed. West Texas Military Academy, San Antonio. Director.
Francis, Noel. b. Temple. Actress.
Fromholz, Steven. b. Temple, 6-8-45. Actor, musician.
Gates, Roy P. b. Houston, 1-19-94. Producer.
George, Phyllis. b. Denton, 6-25-49. TV personality.

Gillespie, A. Arnold (Buddy). b. El Paso, 10-14-99. d. 1978. Special effects, art director.

Gimble, Johnny. b. Tyler, 5-30-26. Actor, musician.

Gomez, Mike. b. Dallas. Actor.

Gonzales-Gonzalez, Pedro. b. Aguilares, 12-21-26. Actor.

Goodrich, Marcus. b. San Antonio. Writer.

Grant, Kathy. b. Houston, 11-25-33. Actress.

Grey, Nan. b. Houston, 7-25-18. Actress.

Griffith, Corinne. b. Texarkana, 11-24-96. d. 7-13-79. Actress.

Guinan, Texas (Mary Louise Cecilia). b. Waco, ca. 1886. d. 11-4-33. Actress.

Gwynne, Anne. b. Waco, 12-10-18. Actress.

Haden, Sara. b. Galveston, 1897. d. 9-15-81. Actress.

Hadley, Reed. b. Petrolia, 1911. d. 12-11-74. Actor.

Hagman, Larry. b. Fort Worth, 9-21-31. Actor.

Hale, Monte. b. San Antonio, 6-8-21. Actor.

Haley, Ted. b. Houston, 10-1-96. Actor.

Hall, James. b. Dallas, 10-22-00. d. 6-7-40. Actor.

Hamblen, Stuart. b. Kellerville, 10-20-08. Singer, songwriter, actor.

Hancock, Lou. b. Fort Worth. Actress.

Hansen, Gunnar. b. Austin. Actor.

Harding, Ann. b. San Antonio, 8-7-01. d. 9-1-81. Actress.

Harrison, Ken. b. Dallas. Director.

Healy, James. b. Houston, 10-1-96. Actor.

Herrmann, Edward. b. Dallas. Actor.

Hillerman, John B. b. Denison, 12-30-32. Actor.

Hooper, Tobe. b. Austin, 1-23-43. Writer, director.

Horsley, Lee. b. Muleshoe, 5-15-55. Actor.

Howard, Jean. b. Dallas, ca. 1908. Actress.

Howard, Susan. b. Marshall. Actress.

Hughes, Howard. b. Houston, 12-24-05. Producer, director.

Hunicutt, Gayle. b. Fort Worth, 2-6-43. Actress.

Huston, John. b. Nevada, MO, 8-5-06. d. 1987. Actor, writer, director.

Hyer, Martha. b. Fort Worth, 8-10-24. Actress.

Hyson, Roberta. b. Dallas, 2-17-05. Actress.

Ivey, Judith. b. El Paso, 9-4-51. Actress.

James, Rian. b. Eagle Pass, 10-3-99. Writer, director.

Janis, Dorothy. b. Dallas, 2-19-10. Actress.

Jenkins, Dan. b. Fort Worth. Writer.

Jennings, Waylon. b. Littlefield, 6-15-37. Singer, actor.

Johnson, J. Brad. b. Fort Worth, 6-18-26. Producer.

Johnson, Rafer. b. Hillsboro, 8-18-35. Actor.

Jones, Beulah Hall. b. San Antonio, 7-28-99. Actress.

Jones, Carolyn. b. Amarillo, 4-28-29. Actress.

Jones, Dickie. b. Snyder, 2-25-27. Actor.

Jones, Tommy Lee. b. San Saba, 9-15-46. Actor.

Keyes, Evelyn. b. Port Arthur, 11-20-19. Actress.

Kibbee, Guy. b. El Paso, 3-6-82. d. 5-24-56. Actor.

King, Charles L. b. Hillsboro, 1-21-95. d. 5-7-57. Actor.

Kristofferson, Kris. b. Brownsville, 6-22-36. Actor, singer.
Lawrance, Jody. b. Fort Worth, 10-19-30. Actress.
Le Maire, William. b. Fort Worth, 12-21-92. Actor.
Lewyn, Louis. b. Houston, 12-18-92. Producer.
Littlefield, Lucien. b. San Antonio, 8-16-95. d. 6-4-60. Actor.
Logan, Jacqueline. b. Corsicana, 11-30-01. Actress.
Logan, Joshua. b. Texarkana, 10-5-08. Director.
Love, Bessie. b. Midland, 9-10-98. Actress.
Lynn, Sharon. b. Weatherford. Actress.
McFarland, George E. ("Spanky"). b. Dallas, 10-2-18. Actor.
McKinney, Florine. b. Mart. Actress.
McMurtry, Larry. b. Wichita Falls, 6-3-36. Screenwriter.
Malick, Terrence. b. Waco, 1945. Director, screenwriter.
Malone, Dorothy. b. Chicago, IL, 1-30-25. Lived in Texas early life, ed. SMU. Actress.
Mandrell, Barbara. b. Houston, 12-25-48. Singer, actress.
Mann, Helen. b. Fort Worth. Actress.
Mansfield, Jayne. b. Bryn Mawr, PA, 4-19-33. Lived in Texas most of early life, attended UT. d. 1967. Actress.
Martin, Mary. b. Weatherford, 12-1-13. Actress.
Martin, Steve. b. Waco, 1945. TV and screenwriter, actor.
Maux, Katharine. b. San Angelo, 1912. Actress.
Meredith, Don. b. Mt. Vernon, 4-10-38. Actor.
Meredith, Lu Anne. b. Dallas, ca. 1913. Actress.
Miller, Ann. b. Chireno, 4-12-23. Actress, dancer.
Miller, Roger. b. Fort Worth, 1-2-36. TV performer, songwriter.
Morris, Gary. b. Fort Worth. Actor, singer.
Moylan, Catherine. b. Dallas, 1910. Actress.
Murphy, Audie. b. Kingston, 6-20-24. d. 5-28-71. Actor.
Neal, Edwin. b. Austin. Actor.
Nelson, Willie. b. Abbott, 4-30-33. Actor, singer.
Nesmith, Michael. b. Houston, 12-30-42. Musician, actor, producer.
O'Brien, Dave (Tex). b. Big Spring, 5-31-12. Actor.
O'Day, Neil. b. Prairie Hill. Actress.
Osborne, Miles (Bud). b. Knox County, 7-20-84. d. 2-2-64. Actor.
O'Toole, Annette. b. Houston, 4-1-52. Actress.
Owens, Buck. b. Sherman, 8-12-29. Singer, actor.
Parker, Fess. b. Fort Worth, 8-16-26. ed. UT. Actor.
Parker, Suzy. b. San Antonio, 10-28-33. Actress.
Patton, Bill. b. Amarillo. Actor.
Paxton, Bill. b. Fort Worth. Actor.
Pepper, Jack. b. Palestine, 6-14-02. Actor.
Perrine, Valerie. b. Galveston, 9-3-44. Actress.
Phillips, Doris. b. San Antonio. Actress.
Phillips, Lou Diamond. b. Dallas. Actor, producer.
Pierce, Evelyn. b. Del Rio, 2-5-08. Actress.
Place, Mary Kay. b. Port Arthur. Actress.
Powers, Lucille. b. San Antonio, 11-18-11. Actress.

Prentiss, Paula. b. San Antonio, 3-4-39. Actress.
Quaid, Dennis. b. Houston, 4-9-54. Actor.
Quaid, Randy. b. Houston, 1953. Actor.
Rash, Steve. b. Dallas. Cameraman, director.
Rashad, Phylicia. b. Houston, 6-17-48. Actress.
Ray, Allene. b. San Antonio, 1901. Actress.
Ray, Helen. b. Fort Stockton, 1879. d. 10-20-65. Actress.
Reed, Rex. b. Fort Worth, 10-20-38. Film critic, actor.
Rennick, Ruth. b. Colorado City, TX. Actress.
Reynolds, Debbie. b. El Paso, 4-1-32. Actress.
Reynolds, Joyce. b. El Paso, 10-7-24. Actress.
Ritter, Tex. b. Murvaul (Panola County), 1-12-05. Actor.
Roarke, Adam. b. Dallas. Actor.
Roberts, Lynn. b. El Paso, 11-22-19. Actress.
Robertson, Willard. b. Runnels, 1-1-86. d. 4-5-48. Actor.
Roddenberry, Eugene Wesley (Gene). b. El Paso, 8-19-21. Writer, producer.
Rodriguez, Johnny. b. Sabinal, 12-10-51. Actor, musician.
Rogers, Ginger. b. Independence, MO, 11-16-11. Lived in Fort Worth as child.
    Started in show business in Texas. Actress, dancer.
Rogers, Kenny. b. Houston, 8-21-38. Actor, singer.
Roquemore, Henry. b. Marshall, 3-13-88. Actor.
Roy, Rosalie. b. Stamford. Actress.
Ryan, Irene. b. 10-17-03. d. 4-26-79. El Paso. Actress.
Saal, William. b. Dallas, 1898. Producer.
Scott, Zachary. b. Austin, 2-24-14. d. 10-3-65. Actor.
Sedgwick, Edward. b. Galveston, 11-7-92. d. 5-7-53. Director, actor.
Sedgwick, Eileen. b. Galveston, 1895. Actress.
Sedgwick, Josie. b. Galveston, 1895. d. 4-30-73. Actress.
Shannon, Cora. b. Illinois, 1-30-79. ed. UT law school. Actress.
Sheridan, Ann. b. Denton, 2-21-15. d. 1967. Actress.
Shrake, Bud. b. Fort Worth. Writer.
Shumate, Harold. b. Austin, 9-7-93. Writer, producer, editor.
Siedow, Jim. b. Houston. Actor.
Singer, Lori. b. Corpus Christi. Actress.
Smith, Jaclyn. b. Houston, 10-26-47. Actress.
Spacek, Sissy. b. Quitman, 12-25-49. Actress.
Sparks, Martha Lee. b. Floydada, 7-14-24. Actress.
Stanley, Kim. b. Tularosa, NM, 2-11-25. ed. UT. Actress.
Starling, Imogene. b. Denton. Writer.
Starr, James A. b. Clarksville, 2-3-02. Writer.
Steele, William. b. Texas. Actor.
Storm, Gale. b. Bloomington, 4-5-22. Actress.
Swazey, Patrick. b. Houston. Actor, dancer.
Tally, Thomas. b. Near Waco, ca. 1866. Director.
Teal, Ray. b. Grand Rapids, 1-12-02. d. 4-2-76. Actor.
Thomas, Henry. b. San Antonio. Actor.
Thurman, Bill. b. Dallas. Actor.
Torn, Rip. b. Temple, 2-6-31. ed. A&M and UT. Actor.

Tubb, Ernest. b. Crisp, 2-9-14. Actor, singer.
Tune, Tommy. b. Wichita Falls, 2-28-39. Film actor, stage musical director.
Turner, Douglas. b. Amarillo. Special effects artist. Son of George Turner.
Turner, George E. b. Burkburnett. Writer, animator, effects.
Vaccaro, Brenda. b. Brooklyn, NY, 11-18-39, raised Dallas. Actress.
Valenti, Jack. b. Houston, 9-5-21. Film executive.
Vidor, King. b. Galveston, 2-8-94. d. 1982. Director.
Vinson, Helen. b. Beaumont, 9-17-07. Actress.
Vokel, Elda. b. Brownwood. Actress.
Walker, Charlotte. b. Galveston, 1878. Actress.
Wallach, Eli. b. Brooklyn, NY, 12-7-15. ed. U.T. Actor.
Wedgeworth, Ann. b. Abilene, 1-21-35. Actress.
Weenik, Annabelle. b. Dallas. Actress.
Wells, Jacqueline. b. Dallas, 8-30-14. Actress.
Whelchel, Lisa. b. Fort Worth, 5-29-63. Actress.
Williams, Guinn (Big Boy). b. Decatur, 4-26-99. d. 6-2-62. Actor.
Williams, JoBeth. b. Houston, 1953. Actress.
Willing, Foy. b. Bosque County, 1915. Actor, musician.
Wills, Bob. b. Kosse, 3-6-05. Actor, singer.
Wills, Chill. b. Seagoville, 7-18-03. d. 12-15-78. Actor.
Wilson, Dooley. b. Tyler, 4-3-94. d. 5-3-53. Actor.
Wilson, Whip. b. Pecos, 6-16-19. d. 10-23-64. Actor.
Wittliff, William. Writer, director.
Wright, Marbeth. b. Houston. Actress.

(By hometown)

ABBOTT
Nelson, Willie. b. 4-30-33. Actor, singer.

ABILENE
Wedgeworth, Ann. b. 1-21-35. Actress.

AMARILLO
Charisse, Cyd. b. 3-8-21. Dancer, actress.
Doran, Ann. b. 10-28-13. Actress.
Jones, Carolyn. b. 4-28-29. Actress.
Patton, Bill. Actor.
Turner, Douglas. Effects artist.

ARLINGTON
Anderson, Andy. Director, writer.
Barrett, Judith. b. 2-2-14. Actress.
Dover, Nancy. b. 2-2-09. Actress.

AUSTIN
Burns, Marilyn. Actress.
Coleman, Dabney. b. 1-3-32. Actor.

Hansen, Gunnar. Actor.
Hooper, Tobe. b. 1-23-43. Writer, director.
King, Joe. b. 2-9-1883. d. 4-11-51. Actor.
Neal, Edwin. Actor.
Scott, Zachary. b. 2-24-14. d. 10-3-65. Actor.
Shumate, Harold. b. 9-7-93. Writer, producer, editor.

BIG SPRING
O'Brien, Dave (Tex). b. 5-31-12. Actor.

BLOOMINGTON
Storm, Gale. b. 4-5-22. Actress.

BOSQUE COUNTY
Willing, Foy. b. 1915. Actor, musician.

BOWIE COUNTY
Blocker, Dan. b. 1929. d. 1972. Actor.

BROWNSVILLE
Kristofferson, Kris. b. 6-22-36. Actor, singer.

BROWNWOOD
Vokel, Elda. Actress.

BURKBURNETT
Turner, George E. Cartoon animator, writer, effects.

CHIRENO
Miller, Ann. b. 4-12-23. Actress, dancer.

CLARKSVILLE
Starr, James A. b. 2-3-02. Writer.

COLORADO CITY
Rennick, Ruth. Actress.

CORPUS CHRISTI
Fawcett, Farrah. b. 2-2-47. Actress.

CORSICANA
Brian, Mary. b. 2-17-08. Actress.
Logan, Jacqueline. b. 11-30-01. Actress.

CRISP
Tubb, Ernest. b. 2-9-14. Musician, actor.

CROCKETT
Arledge, John. b. 3-12-06. ed. UT. Actor.

DALLAS
Ahearn, Thomas J. b. 2-23-04. Writer.
Alexander, Richard. b. 11-18-02. Actor.
Avery, Fred (Tex). b. 1907. d. 8-26-80. Animator.
Benson, Robby. b. 1-21-56. Actor, writer, producer.
Bond, Tommy. b. 9-16-27. Actor.
Buchanan, Larry. Director.

Buetel, Jack. b. 9-5-17. Actor.
Butts, Billy. b. 9-8-19. Actor.
Camp, Joe. b. 1940. Director, producer, screenwriter.
Daniels, Bebe. b. 1-14-01. d. 3-16-71. Actress.
Darnell, Linda. b. 10-16-21. d. 1965. Actress.
Fairchild, Morgan. b. 2-3-50. Actress.
Gomez, Mike. Actor.
Hall, James. b. 10-22-00. d. 6-07-40. Actor.
Harrison, Ken. Director.
Herrmann, Edward. Actor.
Howard, Jean. b. ca. 1908. Actress.
Hyson, Roberta. b. 2-17-05. Actress.
Janis, Dorothy. b. 2-19-10. Actress.
McFarland, George E. ("Spanky"). b. 10-2-18. Actor.
Meredith, Lu Anne. b. ca. 1913. Actress.
Moylan, Catherine. b. 1910. Actress.
Phillips, Lou Diamond. Actor, producer.
Rash, Steve. Cameraman, director.
Roark, Adam. Actor.
Saal, William. b. 1898. Producer.
Thurman, Bill. Actor.
Weenick, Annabelle. Actress.
Wells, Jacqueline. (Julie Bishop) b. 8-30-14. Actress.

DAWSON
Comer, Anjanette. b. 8-7-42. ed. Baylor. Actress.

DECATUR
Williams, Guinn (Big Boy). b. 4-26-99. d. 6-2-62. Actor.

DEL RIO
Pierce, Evelyn. b. 2-5-08. Actress.

DENISON
Hillerman, John B. b. 12-30-32. Actor.

DENTON
George, Phyllis. b. 6-25-49. TV performer.
Sheridan, Ann. b. 2-21-15. d. 1967. Actress.
Starling, Imogene. Writer.

DESDEMONA
Brown, James. b. 3-22-20. Actor.

EAGLE PASS
James, Rian. b. 10-3-99. Writer, director.

EL PASO
Gillespie, A. Arnold (Buddy). b. 10-14-99. d. 1978. Special effects, art director.
Ivey, Judith. b. 9-4-51. Actress.
Kibbee, Guy. b. 3-6-82. d. 5-24-56. Actor.
Reynolds, Debbie. b. 4-1-32. Actress.
Reynolds, Joyce. b. 10-7-24. Actress.

Roberts, Lynn. b. 11-22-19. Actress.
Roddenberry, Eugene Wesley (Gene). b. 8-19-21. Writer, producer.
Ryan, Irene. b. 10-17-03. d. 4-26-79. Actress.

FANNIN COUNTY
Boyd, Bill. b. 9-29-10. Musician, actor.

FLOYDADA
Sparks, Martha Lee. b. 7-14-24. Actress.

FORT STOCKTON
Ray, Helen. b. 1879. d. 10-20-65. Actress.

FORT WORTH
Allen, Bob. Actor.
Ames, Adrienne. b. 8-3-09. d. 5-31-47. Actress.
Buckley, Betty. Actress.
Capshaw, Kate. Actress.
Coleman, Ornette. Composer, actor.
Devore, Dorothy. b. 1899. d. 1976. Actress.
Hagman, Larry. b. 9-21-32. Actor.
Hancock, Lou. Actress.
Hunicutt, Gayle. b. 2-6-43. Actress.
Hyer, Martha. b. 8-10-24. Actress.
Jenkins, Dan. Screenwriter.
Johnson, J. Brad. b. 6-18-26. Producer.
Lawrance, Jody. b. 10-19-30. Actress.
Le Maire, William. b. 12-21-92. Actor.
Mann, Helen. Actress.
Miller, Roger. b. 1-2-36. TV performer, songwriter.
Morris, Gary. Actor, singer.
Parker, Fess. b. 8-16-26. ed. UT. Actor.
Paxton, Bill. Actor.
Reed, Rex. b. 10-20-38. Film critic, actor.
Shrake, Bud. Screenwriter.
Whelchel, Lisa. b. 5-29-63. Actress.

GAINESVILLE
Buck, Frank. b. 3-17-88. d. 3-25-50. Producer, hunter, explorer.
Carewe, Edwin. b. 3-5-1883. d. 1-22-40. Director, producer.

GALVESTON
Dexter, Elliott. b. 1870. d. 1941. Actor.
Haden, Sara. b. 1897. d. 9-15-81. Actress.
Perrine, Valerie. b. 9-3-44. Actress.
Sedgwick, Edward. b. 11-7-92. d. 5-7-53. Director, actor.
Sedgwick, Eileen. b. 1895. Actress.
Sedgwick, Josie. b. 1895. d. 4-30-73. Actress.
Vidor, King. b. 2-8-94. d. 1982. Writer, producer, director.
Walker, Charlotte. b. 1878. Actress.

GOOSE CREEK
Busey, Gary. b. 6-29-44. Actor, musician.

GRAND PRAIRIE
Burkley, Dennis. Actor.

GREENVILLE
Boles, John. b. 10-27-95. d. 2-27-69. Actor, singer.

GROESBECK
Baker, Joe Don. b. 2-12-36. Actor.

HENDERSON
Duncan, Sandy. b. 2-20-46. Actress, singer, dancer.

HEREFORD
Ely, Ron. b. 6-21-38. Actor.

HILLSBORO
Bellamy, Madge. b. 6-30-00. Actress.
Duncan, Tommy. b. 1-11-11. Musician, actor.
Johnson, Rafer. b. 8-18-35. Actor.
King, Charles L. b. 1-21-95. 5-7-57. Actor.

HOUSTON
Allen, Debbie. Actress, dancer.
Barry, Donald (Red). b. 1-11-12. d. 1980. Actor, director.
Brooks, Jean. b. 12-23-16. Actress.
Duvall, Shelley. b. 1949. Actress.
Gates, Roy P. b. 1-19-94. Producer.
Grant, Kathy. b. 11-25-33. Actress.
Grey, Nan. b. 11-25-18. Actress.
Healy, James. b. 10-1-96. Actor.
Hughes, Howard. b. 12-24-05. Producer, director.
Lewyn, Louis. b. 12-18-92. Producer.
Mandrell, Barbara. b. 12-25-48. Singer, actress.
Nesmith, Michael. b. 12-30-42. Musician, actor, producer.
O'Toole, Annette. b. 4-1-53. Actress.
Quaid, Dennis. b. 4-9-54. Actor.
Quaid, Randy. b. 1953. Actor.
Rashad, Phylicia. b. 6-17-48. Actress.
Rogers, Kenny. b. 8-21-38. Actor, singer.
Siedow, Jim. Actor.
Smith, Jaclyn. b. 10-26-47. Actress.
Swazey, Patrick. Actor, dancer.
Valenti, Jack. b. 9-5-21. Film executive.
Vidor, Florence. b. 7-23-95. d. 11-3-77. Actress.
Williams, JoBeth. b. 1953. Actress.
Wright, Marbeth. Actress.

HUNTSVILLE
Forrest, Steve. b. 9-29-24. Actor.

KELLERVILLE
Hamblen, Stuart. b. 10-20-08. Singer, songwriter, actor.

KINGSTON
Murphy, Audie. b. 6-20-24. d. 5-28-71. Actor.

KNOX COUNTY
Osborne, Miles (Bud). b. 7-20-1884. d. 2-2-64. Actor.

KOSSE
Wills, Bob. b. 3-6-05. Actor, singer, musician.

LITTLEFIELD
Jennings, Waylon. b. 6-15-37. Singer, actor.

LUBBOCK
Davis, Mac. b. 1-21-42. Actor, singer, songwriter.

MARSHALL
Howard, Susan. Actress.
Roquemore, Henry. b. 3-13-1888. Actor.

MART
McKinney, Florine. b. ca. 1910. Actress

MIDLAND
Love, Bessie. b. 9-10-98. Actress.

MULESHOE
Horsley, Lee. b. 5-15-55. Actor.

MURVAUL
Ritter, Tex. b. 1-12-05. Actor, singer.

PALESTINE
Pepper, Jack. b. 6-14-02. Actor.

PARIS
Early, Dudley. b. 1-18-03. Writer.

PECOS
Wilson, Whip. b. 6-16-19. d. 10-23-64. Actor.

PETROLIA
Hadley, Reed. b. 1911. d. 12-11-74. Actor.

PLAINVIEW
Carson, Sunset. b. 11-12-22. Actor.

PORT ARTHUR
Keyes, Evelyn. b. 11-20-19. Actress.
Place, Mary Kay. Actress.

POSEY
Dean, Eddie. b. 1910. Actor, singer.

PRAIRIE HILL
O'Day, Nell. Actress.

QUITMAN
Spacek, Sissy. b. 12-25-49. Actress.

RUNNELS
Robertson, Willard. b. 1-1-1886. d. 1948. Actor.

SABINAL
Rodriguez, Johnny. b. 12-10-51. Musician, actor.

SAN ANTONIO
Bates, Florence. b. 4-15-1888. d. 1-31-54. Actress.
Burnett, Carol. b. 4-26-33. Actress.
Collins, Kathleen. Actress.
Cooke, Ray. Actor.
Crawford, Joan. b. 3-23-04. d. 1977. Actress.
Goodrich, Marcus. Writer.
Hale, Monte. b. 6-8-21. Actor.
Harding, Ann. b. 8-7-01. d. 9-1-81. Actress.
Jones, Beulah Hall. b. 7-28-99. Actress.
Littlefield, Lucien. b. 8-16-95. d. 6-4-60. Actor.
Parker, Suzy. b. 10-28-33. Actress.
Phillips, Doris. Actress.
Powers, Lucille. b. 11-18-11. Actress.
Prentiss, Paula. b. 3-4-39. Actress.
Ray, Allene. b. 1901. Actress.
Thomas, Henry. Actor.

SAN SABA
Jones, Tommy Lee. b. 9-15-46. Actor.

SEAGOVILLE
Wills, Chill. b. 7-18-03. d. 12-15-78. Actor.

SETH WARD
Dean, Jimmy. b. 8-10-28. Singer, actor.

SHERMAN
Flowers, Bess. b. 1900. Actress.
Owens, Buck. b. 8-12-29. Actor, singer.

SNYDER
Jones, Dickie. b. 2-25-27. Actor.

STAMFORD
Roy, Rosalie. Actress.

SUMMERVILLE
Broaddus, Milton (Tex). b. 9-16-27. Actor, dancer.

TEMPLE
Francis, Noel. Actress.
Fromholz, Steven. b. 6-8-45. Actor, musician.
Torn, Rip. b. 2-6-31. ed. A&M and UT. Actor.

TEXARKANA
Griffith, Corinne. b. 11-24-96. d. 7-13-79. Actress.
Logan, Joshua. b. 10-5-08. Director.

TIOGA
Autry, Gene. b. 9-29-07. Actor, singer, producer.

TYLER
Gimble, Johnny. b. 5-30-26. Actor, musician.
Wilson, Dooley. b. 4-3-94. d. 5-3-53. Actor.

UVALDE
Evans, Dale. b. 10-31-12. Actress, singer.

WACO
Banton, Travis. b. 8-18-94. Costume designer.
Guinan, Texas (Mary Louise Cecilia). b. ca. 1886. d. 11-4-33. Actress.
Gwynne, Anne. b. 12-10-18. Actress.
Malick, Terrence. b. 1945. Producer, director, screenwriter.
Martin, Steve. b. 1945. Writer, actor.

WAXAHACHIE
Benton, Robert. b. 9-29-32. Screenwriter, director.

WEATHERFORD
Lynn, Sharon. Actress.
Martin, Mary. b. 12-1-13. Actress.

WHARTON
Foote, Horton. b. 3-14-16. Writer.

WICHITA FALLS
McMurtry, Larry. b. 6-3-36. Screenwriter.
Tune, Tommy. b. 2-28-39. Film actor, stage musical director.

BORN OUTSIDE TEXAS
Abraham, F. Murray. b. Pittsburgh, PA, 10-24-39. ed. UT-El Paso. Actor.
Andrews, Dana. b. Collins, MS, 1-1-09. Lived in Texas much of early life. ed. Sam
    Houston State. Actor.
Blakely, Susan. b. Frankfort, Ger., 1950. ed. UT. Actress.
Boone, Pat (Charles Eugene). b. Jacksonville, FL, 6-1-34. Lived Fort Worth, ed.
    North Texas State. Actor, singer.
Boyd, William M. b. Shreveport, LA, 11-29-47. Actor, musician, writer.
Easton, Robert. b. Milwaukee, 11-23-30. ed. UT. Actor.
Fox, Wallace. b. Purcell, OK, 3-9-95. ed. West Texas Military Academy, San An-
    tonio. Director.
Huston, John. b. Nevada, MO, 8-5-06. d. 1987. Actor, writer, director. Started
    professional career while living in Weatherford.
Malone, Dorothy. b. Chicago, IL, 1-30-25. Early life in Dallas. ed. SMU. Actress.
Rogers, Ginger. b. Independence, MO, 11-16-11. Lived in Fort Worth as child.
    Started in show business in Texas. Actress.
Shannon, Cora. b. Illinois, 1-30-79. ed. UT law school. Actress.
Stanley, Kim. b. Tularosa, NM, 2-11-25. ed. UT. Actress.
Teal, Ray. b. Grand Rapids, MI, 1-12-02. d. 4-2-76. ed. UT. Actor.
Vaccaro, Brenda. b. Brooklyn, NY, 11-18-39, raised Dallas. Actress.
Wallach, Eli. b. Brooklyn, NY, 12-7-15. ed. UT. Actor.

Filmography of Selected Artists

GENE AUTRY

1934 — *In Old Santa Fe.* 1935 — *Phantom Empire* (serial), *Tumblin' Tumbleweeds, Melody Trail, Sagebrush Troubadour, The Singing Vagabond, Red River Valley.* 1936 — *Comin' Round the Mountain, Galloping Minstrel, Guns and Guitars, The Singing Cowboy, Oh, Susannah!, Ride, Ranger, Ride.* 1937 — *Git Along Little Doggie, Rootin' Tootin' Rhythm* (or *Rhythm on the Ranch*), *Yodelin' Kid from Pine Ridge, Public Cowboy No. 1, Boots and Saddles, Springtime in the Rockies, Manhattan Merry-Go-Round, Round-Up Time in Texas, The Big Show, The Old Corral* (or, *Texas Serenade*). 1938 — *The Old Barn Dance, Gold Mine in the Sky, The Man From Music Mountain, Rhythm on the Saddle, Western Jamboree, Prairie Moon, Ridin' the Range.* 1939 — *Home on the Prairie, Mexicali Rose, Blue Montana Skies, Mountain Rhythm, Colorado Sunset, In Old Monterey, Rovin' Tumbleweeds.* 1940 — *South of the Border, Shooting High, Rancho Grande, Gaucho Serenade, Carolina Moon, Ride, Tenderfoot, Ride, Melody Ranch, Men With Steel Faces.* 1941 — *Ridin' on a Rainbow, Back in the Saddle, The Singing Hills, Sunset in Wyoming, Under Fiesta Stars, Down Mexico Way, Sierra Sue.* 1942 — *Cowboy Serenade* (or, *Serenade of the West*), *Heart of the Rio Grande, Home in Wyomin', Stardust on the Sage, Call of the Canyon, The Bells of Capistrano.* 1946 — *Sioux City Sue, Range War, Robin Hood in Texas.* 1947 — *Twilight on the Rio Grande, Saddle Pals, Trail to San Antone, The Last Roundup.* 1948 — *Strawberry Roan, Loaded Pistols.* 1949 — *Riders of the Whistling Pines, Guns and Saddles, The Big Sombrero, Rim of the Canyon, Riders in the Sky.* 1950 — *Indian Territory, The Blazing Sun, Cow Town, Beyond the Purple Hills, Mule Train, Sons of New Mexico* (or, *The Brat*). 1951 — *Texans Never Cry, Whirlwind, Silver Canyon, Hills of Utah, Valley of Fire, Gene Autry and the Mounties.* 1952 — *Blue Canadian Rockies, The Old West, Night Stage to Galveston, Apache Country, Wagon Train, Barbed Wire.* 1953 — *On Top of Old Smoky, Saginaw Trail, The Winning of the West, Pack Train, Goldtown Ghost Riders, Last of the Pony Riders.*

Also appeared in television series.

ROBERT BENTON

1967 — *Bonnie and Clyde* (sc). 1970 — *There Was A Crooked Man* (sc). 1972 — *Bad Company* (sc & dir). 1974 — *Oh Calcutta!* (sc). 1977 — *The Late Show* (sc & dir). 1978 — *Superman* (sc). 1979 — *Kramer vs. Kramer* (sc & dir). 1984 — *Places in the Heart* (sc & dir).

GARY BUSEY

1972 — *The Last American Hero.* 1976 — *A Star Is Born, The Gumball Rally.* 1978 — *Straight Time, Big Wednesday, Buddy Holly Story.* 1980 — *Fooling Around.* 1982 — *Barbarosa.* 1984 — *Bear.* 1986 — *Let's Get Harry, The Eye of the Tiger.* 1987 — *Lethal Force.*

Various television appearances.

JOAN CRAWFORD

1925 — *Pretty Ladies, Old Clothes, The Only Thing, Sally, Irene and Mary.* 1926 — *The Boob, Tramp, Tramp, Tramp, Paris.* 1927 — *The Taxi Dancer, Winners of the Wilderness, The Understanding Heart, The Unknown, Twelve Miles Out, Spring Fever.* 1928 — *West Point, Rose-Marie, Across to Singapore, The Law of the Range, Four Walls, Our Dancing Daughters, Dream of Love, The Duke Steps Out, Hollywood Revue*

of 1929, Our Modern Maidens, Untamed. 1930 — *Montana Moon, Our Blushing Brides, Paid.* 1931 — *Dance, Fools, Dance, Laughing Sinners, This Modern Age.* 1932 — *Grand Hotel, Letty Lynton, Rain.* 1933 — *Today We Live, Dancing Lady.* 1934 — *Sadie McKee, Chained, Forsaking All Others.* 1935 — *No More Ladies, I Live My Life.* 1936 — *The Gorgeous Hussy, Love on the Run.* 1937 — *The Last of Mrs. Cheyney, The Bride Wore Red, Mannequin.* 1938 — *The Shining Hour.* 1939 — *The Ice Follies of 1939, The Women.* 1940 — *Strange Cargo, Susan and God.* 1941 — *A Woman's Face, When Ladies Meet.* 1942 — *They All Kissed the Bride, Reunion in France.* 1943 — *Above Suspicion.* 1944 — *Hollywood Canteen.* 1945 — *Mildred Pierce.* 1946 — *Humoresque.* 1947 — *Possessed, Daisy Kenyon.* 1949 — *Flamingo Road, It's a Great Feeling.* 1950 — *The Damned Don't Cry, Harriet Craig.* 1951 — *Goodbye, My Fancy.* 1952 — *This Woman Is Dangerous, Sudden Fear.* 1953 — *Torch Song.* 1954 — *Johnny Guitar.* 1955 — *Female on the Beach, Queen Bee.* 1956 — *Autumn Leaves.* 1957 — *The Story of Esther Costello.* 1959 — *The Best of Everything.* 1962 — *What Ever Happened to Baby Jane?* 1963 — *The Caretakers.* 1964 — *Strait Jacket.* 1965 — *I Saw What You Did.* 1968 — *Berserk.* 1970 — *Trog.*
Numerous television appearances from 1953 through 1972.

BEBE DANIELS
1910 — *The Common Enemy.* 1916 — *An Awful Romance, Luke's Society Mixup, Luke's Movie Muddle.* 1917 — *Lonesome Luke On Tin Can Alley, Lonesome Luke's Honeymoon, Stop! Luke! Listen!, Lonesome Luke's Wild Women, Over the Fence, Pinched, Bliss, Birds of a Feather, Rainbow Island, The Flirt, We Never Sleep.* 1918 — *The Lamb, Here Come the Girls, Fireman Save My Child, An Ozark Romance, Nothing but Trouble.* 1919 — *Young Mr. Jazz, The Marathon, Spring Fever, Just Neighbors, Be My Wife, The Rajah, Soft Money, Bumping Into Broadway, Captain Kidd's Kids, Male and Female, Everywoman.* 1920 — *Why Change Your Wife?, The Dancin' Fool, The 14th Man, You Never Can Tell.* 1921 — *Ducks and Drakes, Two Weeks to Pay, The March Hare, One Wild Week, The Affairs of Anatol, The Speed Girl.* 1922 — *Nancy From Nowhere, North of the Rio Grande, Nice People, Pink Gods, Singed Wings.* 1923 — *The World's Applause, Glimpses of the Moon, His Children's Children, The Exciters.* 1924 — *The Heritage of the Desert, Daring Youth, Unguarded Women, Monsieur Beaucaire, Dangerous Money, Sinners in Heaven, Argentine Love.* 1925 — *Miss Bluebeard, The Crowded Hour, The Manicure Girl, Lovers in Quarantine, Wild Wild Susan, The Splendid Crime.* 1926 — *Miss Brewster's Millions, The Palm Beach Girl, Volcano, The Campus Flirt, Stranded in Paris.* 1927 — *A Kiss in a Taxi, Senorita, Swim Girl Swim, She's a Sheik.* 1928 — *Hot News, The Fifty-Fifty Girl, Take Me Home, Feel My Pulse, What a Night!* 1929 — *Rio Rita.* 1930 — *Love Comes Along, Alias French Gertie, Dixiana, Lawful Larceny.* 1931 — *Reaching for the Moon, My Past, The Maltese Falcon.* 1932 — *Silver Dollar.* 1933 — *42nd Street, Cocktail Hour, Counsellor-at-Law.* 1934 — *Registered Nurse.* 1935 — *Magic Is Magic.* 1939 — *The Return of Dean.* 1941 — *Hi Gang!* 1953 — *Life With the Lyons.* 1955 — *The Lyons in Paris.*

LINDA DARNELL
1939 — *Hotel for Women, Daytime Wife.* 1940 — *Star Dust, Brigham Young, The Mark of Zorro, Chad Hanna.* 1941 — *Blood and Sand, Rise and Shine.* 1942 — *The Loves of Edgar Allan Poe.* 1943 — *City Without Men, The Song of Bernadette* (unbilled, as Virgin Mary). 1944 — *It Happened Tomorrow, Buffalo Bill, Summer Storm, Sweet and*

Lowdown. 1945 — *Hangover Square, The Great John L., Fallen Angel.* 1946 — *Centennial Summer, Anna and the King of Siam, My Darling Clementine.* 1947 — *Forever Amber.* 1948 — *The Walls of Jericho, Unfaithfully Yours.* 1949 — *A Letter to Three Wives, Slattery's Hurricane, Everybody Does It.* 1950 — *No Way Out, Two Flags West.* 1951 — *The Thirteenth Letter, The Guy Who Came Back, The Lady Pays Off.* 1952 — *Saturday Island, Island of Desire, Night Without Sleep, Blackbeard the Pirate.* 1953 — *Donne Probite/Angels of Darkness.* 1954 — *This Is My Love.* 1955 — *Gli Ultimi.* 1956 — *Dakota Incident.* 1957 — *Zero Hour.* 1963 — *El Valle de las Espadas/The Castilian.* 1965 — *Black Spurs.*

FARRAH FAWCETT

1970 — *Myra Breckinridge, Un Homme Qui Me Plait/Love Is a Funny Thing.* 1976 — *Logan's Run.* 1977 — *Somebody Killed Her Husband.* 1979 — *Sunburn, Strictly Business, The Helper.* 1980 — *Saturn 3.* 1981 — *Cannonball Run.* 1986 — *Extremities.*

Made-for-TV movies: 1971 — *The Feminist and the Fuzz.* 1973 — *The Great American Beauty Contest.* 1974 — *The Girl Who Came Gift Wrapped.* 1981 — *Murder in Texas.* 1985 — *The Burning Bed.* 1986 — *The Beate Klarsfeld Story.*

Various television appearances, including "Charlie's Angels" series.

HORTON FOOTE

1962 — *To Kill a Mockingbird.* 1964 — *Baby, The Rain Must Fall.* 1966 — *The Chase.* 1967 — *Hurry Sundown.* 1983 — *Tender Mercies.* 1985 — *1918, The Trip to Bountiful.* 1986 — *On Valentine's Day.* 1987 — *Courtship.*

Twenty or more teleplays.

LARRY HAGMAN

1964 — *Ensign Pulver, Fail Safe.* 1965 — *The Cavern, In Harm's Way.* 1966 — *The Group.* 1970 — *Up in the Cellar.* 1972 — *Beware! The Blob* (also directed). 1974 — *Harry and Tonto.* 1975 — *Stardust.* 1976 — *Jugs and Speed, The Big Bus.* 1977 — *The Eagle Has Landed.* 1978 — *Superman.* 1981 — *S.O.B.*

Numerous television appearances, including series "I Dream of Jeannie" and "Dallas."

HOWARD HUGHES

1926 — *Everybody's Acting.* 1927 — *Two Arabian Nights.* 1928 — *The Mating Call, The Racket.* 1930 — *Hell's Angels.* 1931 — *The Front Page.* 1932 — *Cock of the Air, Sky Devils, Scarface.* 1933 — *Bombshell.* 1941-43-47-50 — *The Outlaw.* 1946-50 — *Vendetta.* 1947 — *Mad Wednesday.* 1951 — *His Kind of Woman.*

KRIS KRISTOFFERSON

1971 — *The Last Movie* (bit; also music). 1972 — *Cisco Pike* (title role; also music). 1973 — *Pat Garrett and Billy the Kid, The Gospel Road* (singing own songs), *Blume in Love* (also song). 1974 — *Bring Me the Head of Alfredo Garcia.* 1975 — *Alice Doesn't Live Here Anymore.* 1976 — *The Sailor Who Fell from Grace With the Sea, Vigilante Force, A Star Is Born.* 1977 — *Semi-Tough.* 1978 — *Convoy.* 1984 — *Flashpoint.* 1985 — *Songwriter.*

Also has appeared in several movies made for television.

AUDIE MURPHY

1948 — *Beyond Glory, Texas, Brooklyn and Heaven.* 1949 — *Bad Boy.* 1950 — *Sierra, The Kid from Texas, Kansas Raiders.* 1951 — *The Red Badge of Courage, The Cimarron Kid.* 1952 — *The Duel at Silver Creek.* 1953 — *Gunsmoke, Column South, Tumble-*

weed. 1954 — *Ride Clear of Diablo, Drums Across the River, Destry.* 1955 — *To Hell and Back.* 1956 — *World in My Corner, Walk the Proud Land.* 1957 — *The Guns of Fort Petticoat, Joe Butterfly, Night Passage.* 1958 — *The Quiet American, Ride a Crooked Trail, The Gun Runners.* 1959 — *No Name on the Bullet, The Wild and the Innocent, Cast a Long Shadow.* 1960 — *Hell Bent for Leather, The Unforgiven, Seven Ways from Sundown.* 1961 — *Posse from Hell, Battle at Bloody Beach.* 1962 — *Six Black Horses.* 1963 — *Showdown, Gunfight at Comanche Creek.* 1964 — *The Quick Gun, Bullet for a Badman, Apache Rifles.* 1965 — *Arizona Raiders.* 1966 — *Gunpoint, Trunk to Cairo, The Texican.* 1967 — *40 Guns to Apache Pass.* 1971 — *A Time for Dying.*

Also appeared on television briefly.

WILLIE NELSON

1979 — *The Electric Horseman.* 1980 — *Honeysuckle Rose.* 1981 — *Thief.* 1982 — *Barbarosa.* 1985 — *The Songwriter.* 1987 — *The Red Headed Stranger.*

Numerous television appearances.

TEX RITTER

1936 — *Song of the Gringo.* 1937 — *Arizona Days, Trouble in Texas, Hittin' the Trail, Sing, Cowboy, Sing, Riders of the Rockies, Tex Rides with the Boy Scouts, Mystery of the Hooded Horsemen.* 1938 — *Frontier Town, Rollin' Plains, The Utah Trail, Starlight Over Texas, Where the Buffalo Roam.* 1939 — *Song of the Buckaroo, Sundown on the Prairie, Riders of the Frontier, Rollin' Westward, Roll, Wagons, Roll, Down the Wyoming Trail, Man from Texas, Westbound Stage.* 1940 — *Rhythm of the Rio Grande, Pals of the Silver Sage, The Golden Trail, The Cowboy from Sundown, Take Me Back to Oklahoma, Rainbow Over the Range, Arizona Frontier.* 1941 — *Rolling Home to Texas, Riding the Cherokee Trail, The Pioneers, King of Dodge City, Roaring Frontiers, Lone Star Vigilantes, Bullets for Bandits, The Devil's Trail, North of the Rockies, Prairie Gunsmoke, Vengeance of the West.* 1942 — *Deep in the Heart of Texas, Little Joe the Wrangler, The Old Chisholm Trail, Raiders of San Joaquin.* 1943 — *The Lone Star Trail, Tenting Tonight on the Old Camp Ground, Cheyenne Roundup, Frontier Badmen, Arizona Trail.* 1944 — *Marshal of Gunsmoke, Oklahoma Raiders, Cowboy Canteen, Gangsters of the Frontier, Dead or Alive, The Whispering Skull, Marked for Murder.* 1945 — *Enemy of the Law, Three in the Saddle, Frontier Fugitives, Flaming Bullets.* 1950 — *Holiday Rhythm.* 1954 — *The Cowboy* (narrator). 1955 — *Apache Ambush.* 1956 — *Down Liberty Road.* 1966 — *What's the Country Coming To?* (narrator), *Girl from Tobacco Road, Nashville Rebel.* 1971 — *The Nashville Sound.* 1972 — *The Nashville Story, Music City, U.S.A.* (narrator).

GINGER ROGERS

1930 — *Young Man of Manhattan, The Sap From Syracuse, Queen High, Follow the Leader.* 1931 — *Honor Among Lovers, The Tip-Off, Suicide Fleet.* 1932 — *Carnival Boat, The Tenderfoot, The Thirteenth Guest, Hat Check Girl, You Said a Mouthful.* 1933 — *Broadway Bad, 42nd Street, Gold Diggers of 1933, Professional Sweetheart, A Shriek in the Night, Don't Bet on Love, Sitting Pretty, Flying Down to Rio, Chance at Heaven.* 1934 — *20 Million Sweethearts, Rafter Romance, Finishing School, Change of Heart, Upper World, The Gay Divorcee.* 1935 — *Romance in Manhattan, Roberta, Star of Midnight, Top Hat, In Person.* 1936 — *Follow the Fleet, Swing Time.* 1937 — *Shall We Dance, Stage Door.* 1938 — *Vivacious Lady, Having a Wonderful Time, Carefree.* 1939 — *The Story of Vernon and Irene Castle, Bachelor Mother, Fifth Avenue Girl.*

1940 — *Primrose Path, Lucky Partners.* 1941 — *Kitty Foyle, Tom, Dick and Harry.* 1942 — *Roxie Hart, The Major and the Minor, Tales of Manhattan, Once Upon a Honeymoon.* 1944 — *Lady in the Dark, Tender Comrade.* 1945 — *I'll Be Seeing You, Weekend at the Waldorf.* 1946 — *Heartbeat, Magnificent Doll.* 1947 — *It Had to be You.* 1949 — *The Barkleys of Broadway.* 1950 — *Perfect Strangers.* 1951 — *Storm Warning, The Groom Wore Spurs.* 1952 — *We're Not Married, Dreamboat, Monkey Business.* 1954 — *Forever Female, Black Widow, Twist of Fate.* 1955 — *Tight Spot.* 1956 — *Teenage Rebel, The First Traveling Saleslady.* 1957 — *Oh, Men! Oh, Women!.* 1965 — *Harlow.* 1964 — *The Confession* (not released).

ANN SHERIDAN

As Clara Lou Sheridan: 1934 — *Search for Beauty, Bolero, Come On Marines!, Murder at the Vanities, Kiss and Make Up, Shoot the Works, The Notorious Sophie Lang, Ladies Should Listen, Wagon Wheels, Mrs. Wiggs of the Cabbage Patch, College Rhythm, You Belong to Me, Limehouse Blues.* 1935 — *Enter Madame, Home on the Range, Rumba.*

As Ann Sheridan: 1935 — *Behold My Wife, Car 99, Rocky Mountain Mystery, Mississippi, The Glass Key, The Crusades, Red Blood of Courage, Fighting Youth.* 1936 — *Sing Me a Love Song.* 1937 — *Black Legion, The Great O'Malley, San Quentin, Wine Women and Horses, The Footloose Heiress, Alcatraz Island.* 1938 — *She Loved a Fireman, The Patient in Room 18, Mystery House, Cowboy From Brooklyn, Little Miss Thoroughbred, Letter of Introduction, Broadway Musketeers, Angels With Dirty Faces.* 1939 — *They Made Me a Criminal, Dodge City, Naughty but Nice, Winter Carnival, Indianapolis Speedway, Angels Wash Their Faces.* 1940 — *Castle on the Hudson, It All Came True, Torrid Zone, They Drive by Night, City for Conquest.* 1941 — *Honeymoon for Three, Navy Blues.* 1942 — *The Man Who Came to Dinner, Kings Row, Juke Girl, Wings for the Eagle, George Washington Slept Here.* 1943 — *Edge of Darkness, Thank Your Lucky Stars* (cameo). 1944 — *Shine On Harvest Moon, The Doughgirls.* 1946 — *One More Tomorrow.* 1947 — *Nora Prentiss, The Unfaithful.* 1948 — *The Treasure of the Sierra Madre* (unbilled cameo), *Silver River, Good Sam.* 1949 — *I Was a Male War Bride.* 1950 — *Stella, Woman on the Run.* 1952 — *Steel Town, Just Across the Street.* 1953 — *Take Me to Town, Appointment in Honduras.* 1956 — *Come Next Spring, The Opposite Sex.* 1957 — *Woman and the Hunter.*

Also appeared on television.

SISSY SPACEK

1970 — *Trash* (extra). 1972 — *Prime Cut.* 1973 — *Badlands.* 1976 — *Carrie.* 1977 — *Three Women, Welcome to L.A.* 1980 — *Coal Miner's Daughter, Heart Beat.* 1981 — *Raggedy Man.* 1982 — *Missing.* 1984 — *The River.* 1985 — *Marie.* 1986 — *Violets Are Blue, 'night, Mother, Crimes of the Heart.*

TV films: 1973 — *Ginger in the Morning, The Girls of Huntingdon House.* 1974 — *The Migrants.* 1975 — *Katharine.* 1978 — *Verna — USO Girl.*

RIP TORN

1957 — *Time Limit.* 1959 — *Pork Chop Hill.* 1961 — *King of Kings.* 1962 — *Sweet Bird of Youth, Hero's Island.* 1963 — *Critic's Choice.* 1965 — *The Cincinnati Kid.* 1966 — *You're a Big Boy Now.* 1967 — *Beach Red.* 1968 — *Sol Madrid, Beyond the Law.* 1969 — *Coming Apart.* 1970 — *Tropic of Cancer.* 1971 — *Maidstone.* 1972 — *Slaughter.* 1973 — *Payday.* 1974 — *Crazy Joe.* 1976 — *Birch Interval, The Man Who Fell to Earth.* 1977 — *Nasty Habits, On the Line* (narrator). 1978 — *Coma.* 1979 — *Heartland, The Seduction of Joe Tynan.* 1980 — *First Family, The Private Files of*

J. Edgar Hoover, One Trick Pony. 1982 — *A Stranger Is Watching, Beastmaster, Jinxed, Airplane II: The Sequel.* 1983 — *Cross Creek.* 1984 — *Misunderstood, Flashpoint, City Heat.* 1985 — *Songwriter.*

TV movies: 1973 — *The President's Plane Is Missing.* 1974 — *Attack on Terror: The FBI vs. the Ku Klux Klan.* 1978 — *Betrayal, Steel Cowboy.* 1979 — *A Shining Season.* 1980 — *Sophia Loren: Her Own Story.* 1984 — *Cat on a Hot Tin Roof, When She Says No.* 1985 — *The Execution.*

KING VIDOR

1919 — *The Turn in the Road* (also sc), *Better Times* (also sc), *The Other Half* (also sc), *Poor Relations* (also sc), *The Jack-Knife Man* (also prod, co-sc). 1920 — *The Family Honor* (also prod). 1921 — *Love Never Dies* (also prod), *The Sky Pilot* (also co-prod). 1922 — *Woman, Wake Up* (also prod), *Dusk to Dawn* (also prod), *The Real Adventure* (also prod), *Wild Oranges* (also sc). 1923 — *Conquering the Woman* (also prod), *Alice Adams* (also prod), *Peg o' My Heart, The Woman of Bronze, Three Wise Fools* (also sc), *Happiness.* 1924 — *His Hour, Wine of Youth, Wife of the Centaur.* 1925 — *Proud Flesh* (also co-prod), *The Big Parade* (also prod). 1926 — *La Boheme* (also prod), *Bardelys the Magnificent* (also prod). 1928 — *The Crowd* (also prod, co-sc), *Show People* (also co-prod), *The Patsy.* 1929 — *Hallelujah* (also prod, sc). 1930 — *Not So Dumb* (also co-prod), *Billy the Kid.* 1931 — *Street Scene, The Champ* (also prod). 1932 — *Bird of Paradise, Cynara.* 1933 — *The Stranger's Return* (also prod). 1934 — *Our Daily Bread* (also prod). 1935 — *The Wedding Night, So Red the Rose.* 1936 — *The Texas Rangers* (also prod, co-sc). 1937 — *Stella Dallas.* 1938 — *The Citadel.* 1940 — *Northwest Passage, Comrade X.* 1941 — *H. M. Pulham, Esq.* (also prod, co-sc). 1944 — *An American Romance* (also prod, story). 1946 — *Duel in the Sun.* 1948 — *A Miracle Can Happen.* 1949 — *The Fountainhead, Beyond the Forest.* 1951 — *Lightning Strikes Twice.* 1952 — *Japanese War Bride, Ruby Gentry* (also co-prod). 1955 — *Man Without a Star.* 1956 — *War and Peace* (also co-sc). 1959 — *Solomon and Sheba* (also executive prod).

Bibliography

Below is a partial listing of sources consulted in the preparation of this book which may be of interest to readers. Some serial publications that I used may not be available in any except specialized libraries. Examples are early issues of *Photoplay Magazine, The Motion Picture Herald,* and the annual publication of *The Motion Picture Almanac.*

Allgood, Jill. *Bebe & Ben.* London: Robert Hale & Co., 1975.

Bacon, James. *Made in Hollywood.* New York: Warner Books, 1977.

Cary, Diana Serra. *Hollywood Children.* Boston: Houghton Mifflin, 1979.

Davis, Bette. *The Lonely Life.* New York: G. P. Putnam's Sons, 1962.

De Mille, Cecil B. *Autobiography of Cecil B. De Mille.* Prentice-Hall, 1959.

Drossnig, Michael. *Citizen Hughes.* New York: Holt, Rinehart, Winston, 1985.

Eells, George. *Ginger, Loretta, & Irene Who?* New York: G. P. Putnam's Sons, 1976.

————. *Hedda & Louella.* New York: G. P. Putnam's Sons, 1982.

Flynn, Charles, and Todd McCarthy. *King of the Bs.* New York: E.P. Dutton, 1975.

Geist, Kenneth L. *Pictures Will Talk.* New York: Charles Scribner's Sons, 1978.

Guiles, Fred Lawrence. *Legend: The Life and Death of Marilyn Monroe.* New York: Stein & Day, 1984.

Gussow, Mel. *Darryl Zanuck.* New York: Doubleday & Co., 1971.

Higham, Charles. *Bette.* New York: Macmillan Publishing Co., 1981.

————. *Celebrity Circus.* New York: Delacorte Press, 1979.

————. *Errol Flynn: The Untold Story.* New York: Dell Publishing Co., 1981.

Hollywood Reporter.

Huston, John. *An Open Book.* New York: Alfred A. Knopf, 1980.

Keyes, Evelyn. *Scarlett O'Hara's Younger Sister.* New York: Fawcett Crest Books, 1977.

Kistler, Ron. *I Caught Flys For Howard Hughes.* Chicago: Playboy Press, 1976.

Logan, Joshua. *Josh.* New York: Delacorte Press, 1976.

Loos, Anita. *A Girl Like I.* New York: Viking Press, 1966.

————. *Kiss Hollywood Goodbye.* New York: Viking Press, 1974.

Love, Bessie. *To Hollywood, from Love.* London: Elm Tree Books, 1977.

Martin, Mary. *My Heart Belongs.* New York. William Morrow Co., 1976.

Miller, Ann, and Norma Lee Browning. *Miller's High Life.* New York: Doubleday & Co., 1972.

Monaco, James. *American Film Now*. New York: Oxford University Press, 1979.

Mordden, Ethan. *Movie Star*. New York: St. Martin's Press, 1983.

Motion Picture Almanac, 1922 —

Motion Picture Herald, 1915 —

Pirie, David, ed. *Anatomy of the Movies*. New York: Macmillan Pub. Co., 1981.

Rothel, David. *The Singing Cowboys*. New Jersey: A.S. Barnes, 1978.

St. Johns, Adela Rogers. *Love, Laughter, & Tears*. New York: Doubleday & Co., 1978.

Schulberg, Budd. *Moving Pictures*. New York: Stein and Day, Briarcliff Manor, 1981.

Sexton, Martha. *Jayne Mansfield*. Boston: Houghton Mifflin, 1975.

Shepherd, Donald, and Robert Slatzer. *Bing Crosby — The Hollow Man*. New York: St. Martin's Press, 1981.

Swanson, Gloria. *Swanson on Swanson*. New York: Simon and Schuster, 1980.

Swindell, Larry. *The Last Hero*. New York: Doubleday & Co., 1980.

Thomas, Bob. *Joan Crawford*. New York: Simon and Schuster, 1978.

Thomas, Tony. *Howard Hughes in Hollywood*. Secaucus, NJ: Citadel Press, 1985.

Townsend, Charles R. *San Antonio Rose*. Urbana: Univ. of Illinois Press, 1976.

Variety. (Daily)

Vidor, King. *A Tree Is A Tree*. London: Garland Publishing, Inc., 1977. (Reprint of 1953 edition.)

Wilkerson, Tichi, and Marcie Borie. *The Hollywood Reporter*. New York: Arlington House, Inc., 1984.

F. Murray Abraham

Debbie Allen

Gene Autry

Robert Benton

Dan Blocker

Pat Boone

Betty Buckley

Carol Burnett

Gary Busey

Sunset Carson

Cyd Charisse

Dabney Coleman

Joan Crawford

Bebe Daniels

Linda Darnell

Sandy Duncan

Shelley Duvall

Dale Evans

Morgan Fairchild

Farrah Fawcett

Kathy Grant

Larry Hagman

John Hillerman

Lee Horsley

Susan Howard

Howard Hughes

John Huston

Carolyn Jones

Tommy Lee Jones

Kris Kristofferson

Terrence Malick

Dorothy Malone

Jayne Mansfield

Mary Martin

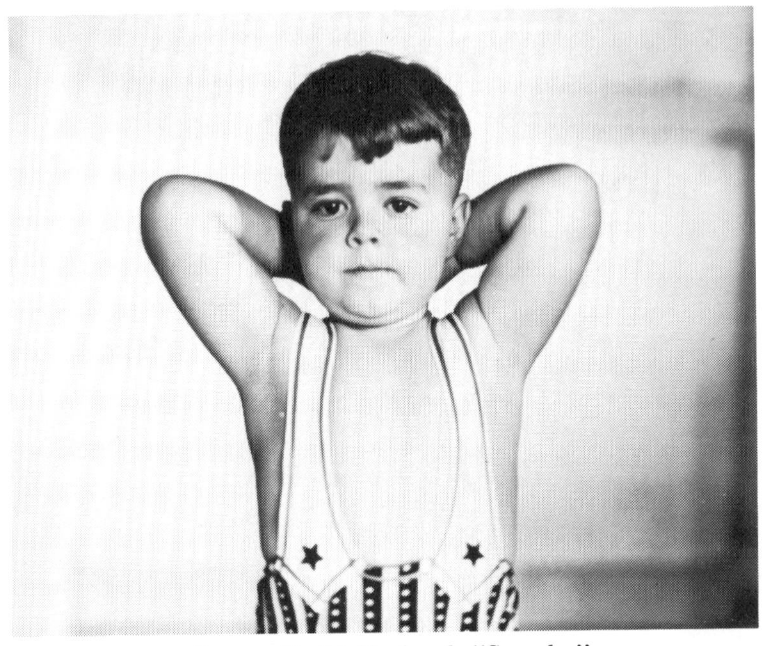

George E. McFarland, "Spanky"

Ann Miller

Audie Murphy

Willie Nelson

Fess Parker

Debbie Reynolds

Tex Ritter

Ginger Rogers

Kenny Rogers

Zachary Scott

Ann Sheridan

Jaclyn Smith

Sissy Spacek

Gale Storm

Rip Torn

Florence Vidor

King Vidor

Chill Wills

Index